superdate

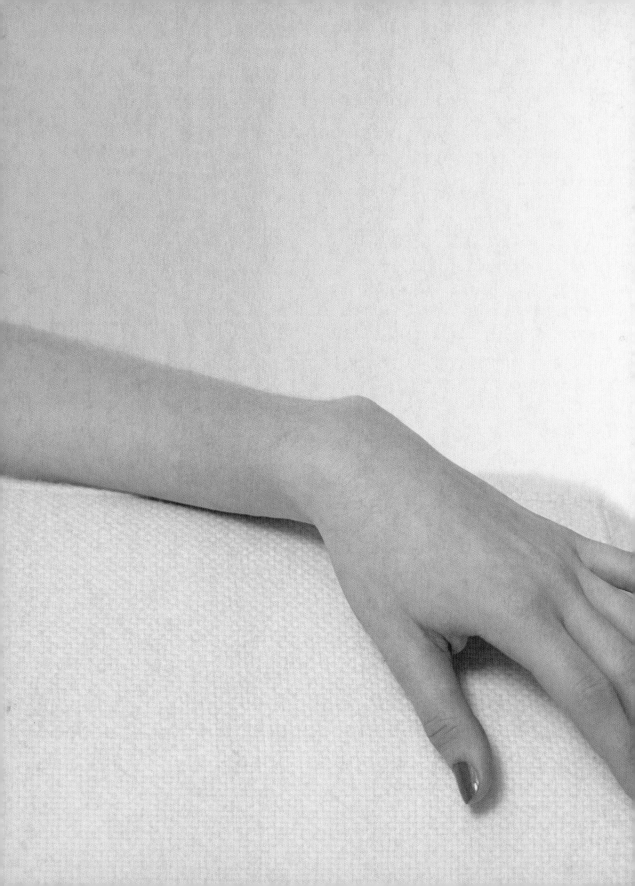

superdate

tracey cox

photography by russell sadur

DK

A Dorling Kindersley Book

LONDON, NEW YORK, MUNICH, MELBOURNE, DELHI

Design
XAB Design
Senior Editor
Peter Jones
Senior Art Editor
Hannah Moore
Managing Art Editor
Emma Forge

DTP Designers
Jackie Plant, Traci Salter
Production Controller
Kevin Ward
Production Manager
Lauren Britton
Jacket Editor
Carrie Love

Publishing Director
Corinne Roberts
Art Director
Carole Ash

First published in
Great Britain in 2005
by Dorling Kindersley Limited,
80 Strand, London WC2R 0RL

A Penguin Company

2 4 6 8 10 9 7 5 3 1

A CIP catalogue record for this book is available from
the British Library.

ISBN 1 4053 0706 4

Reproduced by GRB, Italy
Printed and bound by Star Standard, Singapore

see our complete catalogue at
www.dk.com

contents

"People form 90 per cent of their impression of you in the first 90 seconds"

"The prime purpose of *superdate* is to turn you into one"

"get ready
to get
noticed..."

This is a book about body language and how it can help you be more successful in relationships. It's primarily aimed at singles looking for love, but quite frankly it's useful to anyone who wants to get on better with people in any situation. There are tips for couples too – loads on how to "read" your partner to interpret what they're really thinking and feeling (chapter five is especially dedicated to you!) As with all my books, *superdate* is written from a heterosexual point of view but it applies equally to gay or lesbian relationships. My apologies (again), for not covering the myriad of partnerships out there – it was done purely for simplicity's sake. I toyed with the idea of a separate chapter on gay and lesbian body language but I honestly don't think it's markedly different from straights. Most gay people send the same signals to attract a partner as straights do. The only difference being that the partner you're aiming the signals at, happens to be of the same sex.

The prime purpose of *superdate* is to turn you into one. What you might find odd, given the title, is the lack of chapters on pick-up-lines, what to wear, and where to go. The stuff you find in most dating books isn't covered here because, while all those things are important, the key to your attractiveness and chances of finding a deliciously decadent dalliance is the ability to send and receive clear signals.

So the focus of *superdate* is on body language. Most relationships are formed or dismissed within the first five minutes of meeting. We rely mainly on body language to decide who we like and who we don't because (boring buggers that we are) most initial conversations centre around small talk and trivia. With no real verbal clues of character, we're forced to depend on deciphering unspoken signals. There never was a truer saying than "actions speak louder than words"!

To get the most from this book, it's best to read it on two levels: to check your own body language (am I sending clear signals?) and to decode the subliminal signals people send you. That way you can make quick, informed choices about potential partners based on the little information and little time that's usually available. Once you've done that and are skipping off into the sunset or slamming the door of the nearest bedroom with somebody lovely, the book is useful to help constantly monitor your new relationship, so both of you end up happy ever after!

"People look good at the beginning of relationships **because we want them to look good**"

Keep your eyes open, especially in the beginning, and listen to your gut instinct: this is the best advice I could give anyone looking for a healthy, happy relationship (and that applies to a three-week throw-each-other-up-against-the-fridge flingette as well as the thirty-year, share-the-denture-glass variety). First impressions stick with us because they're nearly always right!! So if some (boringly) sensible part of your brain seems to be constantly nudging you away from lustful fantasies about Mr. or Miss Seemingly Perfect, pay attention. They probably aren't.

That "not sure but don't know why" feeling is almost certainly your subconscious cleverly and cautiously analysing their body language and other subtler signals. Now if a fab shag is all you're after, by all means jump straight in there (with condom packet ripped open). If you're after more, be warned. Your body might be in for a treat but your poor old heart might not. If you've been hurt before and want to play it ultrasafe, listen to your instincts and follow these three ground rules:

• **Pay special attention around date three:** that's when the best-behaviour mask slips and the real person emerges.

• **Introduce them to a friend you trust after the fifth date:** that's long enough for you to make up your own mind but not so long you can't let go if you've missed some glaring, disastrous fault.

• **Keep 30 per cent back for the first three months:** like a protective best friend, a small part of you should stay objective. Run through a checklist to make sure this person is all they seem.

"A bad habit can be changed in 21 days"

A new habit can be learned a lot faster! So while initially it may feel uncomfortable to rethink the way you relate to potential partners, the good news is it's all gain and no pain after just three weeks! Hang in there!

"Get the signals right
and you'll clean up at speed-dating"

Instantly fix any body language that is obviously off-putting by doing two things: move from "closed" to "open" posture and do a consistency check. Closed body language is anything that makes you look "folded in". Crossed arms or legs, a lowered head, refusing to meet people's eyes, curling the body into a ball, hunching shoulders – all make us look unapproachable, cold, and closed to any friendly overtures. Switch to "open" posture and look calm, confident, and friendly simply by uncrossing everything, pulling your shoulders back, and looking people in the eye. Also check everything about you "matches", that the way you are speaking matches your body language. It's no good talking friendly if your body is saying something else. The most popular people are those who make sense to us. Their clothes, body language, words, and voice are all consistent. We like surprises but if someone's *too* contradictory, it's simply confusing.

Sending the right signals?

You could study this book, memorise it cover to cover, become a veritable whiz at deciphering body language, but still end up desperately dateless. How? By forgetting to check your own body language. Even more important than learning how to read others is to be happy with the signals you're sending. Sometimes, the impression we think we're making is a spaceship ride away from reality. Even if you're 150 per cent positive your perception of yourself matches what others think of you, indulge me. At least skim through the following…

• **Listen to yourself** How's the tone, speed, volume of your voice? Do you overuse words, have annoying pet phrases, does every sentence start with "I"? Would *you* like to listen to you?

• **Tape yourself** Most people hate watching themselves on film. Why? Because our memory of how we looked and acted usually bears no comparison to the person staring back at us. Once you've got over the I-can't-believe-I-was-that-sloshed/-silly/-fat part, study the evidence. Look for habits, mannerisms, speech patterns, listening skills, the emotions shown on your face, how you stand, sit, and walk. If you don't have a tape, make one. Set up a camera in a room and simply chat to a friend about anything at all – just keep it going for about half an hour.

• **Look in a mirror** Walk up to it with your eyes shut, picture yourself at a party, chatting to strangers, assume a pose that feels natural, then open your eyes. Look at your posture. What's happening with your arms, hands, legs, feet? What about your facial expression? What would you think if you saw you? Repeat the exercise using a chair to see how you sit, then check out your walk. Ask a close (but honest) friend if their image of you fits your own or if there are things you could improve.

• **Refine, but resist the urge to completely rebuild** Our initial reaction to seeing ourselves clearly is usually "Yuk!!" This is normal. Unless you really don't like what you see and others agree you need to make drastic changes, stick to polishing yourself around the edges. Stay true to the core of who you are and others will be more accepting of changes you do make.

"Check you match: clothes, words and actions should all be consistent"

"Don't do anything
without reading
this first!"

There are two crucial pieces of information you need to be a superdate and to get yourself one: you need to understand body language believability and apply the "Rule of Four". Without the Rule of Four, you'll be jumping to all sorts of bizarre conclusions as you're trying to read potential partners. Without an understanding of body language believability, you won't know what to do if you're getting mixed messages.

Let's start with the Rule of Four. The basic premise: don't ever judge on one thing alone. Think of each clue, signal, or gesture someone sends you as a word in a sentence. While one word alone can make sense ("help"), it can completely change meaning when put into context ("you just can't get good help these days"). To get the full picture, look for other "words" to build a sentence – look for "clusters" of

body language. Sitting with your arms crossed often means you're feeling huffy and defensive. But it can also mean it's bloody freezing or you're conscious of your tummy after scoffing a gigantic bag of crisps! The Rule of Four stops you jumping to silly conclusions because it insists you always look for at least four body language signals, all happening simultaneously and all pointing to the same conclusion, before making a judgement call. If someone has their arms crossed, they're scowling, have stepped backward to create space between you, and their lips are tightly pressed together, it's a fairly safe bet they're a tad on the prickly side.

Body language believability dictates that if someone is sending you conflicting signals – they're smiling but both feet are tightly crossed and tucked under their chair (insecurity) – you should believe the lower part of the body. The farther away from the face it is, the less aware the person is of making a gesture. Most of us are face-focused and aware of assuming the "correct" facial expression, plenty are conscious of what their hands are doing or saying, but few people think to control their feet or leg signals. Autonomic signals – things like sweating and pupil dilation – are out of our control so highest on the believability scale. Our trunk posture is also a good predictor: it's difficult for an excited person to slump, and hard for a bored person to keep their body straight. Legs and feet are also trustworthy. Think about what you're seeing: the more conscious the person is of making the gesture, the less believable it is.

"Science can help you make someone fall in love with you"

1

thesignals

Worst way to stand: with "closed" body language. Uncross and unfold everything!

Slumped shoulders Permanently rounded, slouched shoulders are a sign of constant disappointment and/or shouldering a heavy burden. Shoulders raised high and forward mean you're anxious, hostile, or protective.

Fast fix Pull your shoulders up to your ears, then roll them back down your back. You'll look confident and it makes them appear broader, suggesting strength. Remember the shoulder-padded 80s?

Crossed arms and crossed ankles Cross anything – even loosely – and you'll appear "closed". Standing with locked ankles, like this, is the mental equivalent of "biting your lip". You're holding back negative thoughts.

Fast fix Unfold your arms. Stand with feet a few inches apart rather than heels snapped together. You'll feel more stable and grounded and appear open and approachable.

how not to stand

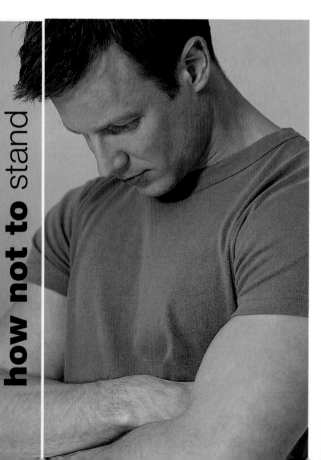

The way we hold ourselves reflects our past, our personality, and our attitude to life. People form 90 per cent of their opinion about you in the first 90 seconds and your posture is a crucial giveaway. The higher you hold yourself, the higher your self-esteem. Transform from timid to take-me-seriously simply by standing tall and making eye contact.

Direct, steady eye contact Our eyes reveal all our emotions. The more you look someone in the eye, letting them see all your secrets, the more confident, attractive, and truthful you seem.

Hand on hip This is a *readiness* gesture – something people do when they're ready to "get things done". (75 per cent of executives stand like this within an hour in a competitive situation.) Do it and you'll appear enthusiastic and successful.

"Want to be seen as confident, sexy, and a high achiever? Stand like this"

Weight on one leg When we're relaxed and confident – usually with people we consider equal or "below" us – we shift our weight so it's distributed more comfortably. Legs and arms cease to be symmetrical and we'll stand with our weight on one hip.

how to stand

Don't walk like this.
Sad and depressed

You can get a strong sense of the type of person someone is, by mimicking the way they move through life. Happy, ambitious people walk fast toward their imagined goals. No purpose and nowhere to go? Chances are they'll walk slowly and shuffle rather than stride.

Eyes down Look down and you're probably feeling it. Look straight ahead and you look to the future. Keeping your head high also keeps shoulders back and tummy in – if your head sags, everything else flops.

Hands shoved in pockets Loose, swinging arms symbolize a soaring heart, hands buried in pockets suggest a need to hide. Any time you hide your palms, you risk looking secretive and dodgy.

Dragging the feet The lighter the step, the lighter the heart. Happy people "bounce" and lift their feet high, as though they were made of air, rather than lead.

how not to walk

"Fast fix: look ahead not down, square your shoulders"

Walk with an even pace with a slight bounce, tilt your pelvis forward, hold your head high, half smile, and look at other people. You'll feel more involved in the world by seeing what's going on around you, not to mention look more confident. All will get you noticed and to first base!

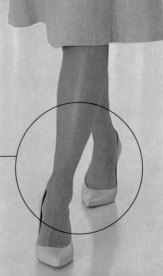

Relaxed fingers
Don't curl hands into fists, let them fall naturally – slightly cupped with fingers curved. When you walk, allow them to sway as a natural result of your body movement.

Swinging your hips Women have wider pelvic girdles and their pelvis rolls more, causing their hips to swing. Exaggerate the swivel and you exaggerate your femininity. Swinging hips – a sign of flexibility – makes both sexes look young.

Feet walking a central, straight line
If you're female, every time you place a foot forward, put it dead centre instead of to the side. "Toeing the line" is an old catwalk trick that forces a wiggle.

how to walk

Would you approach this guy? The answer is no. He looks both cocky and unsettled

● **Straddling a chair** This pose sends contradictory signals. By straddling the chair and placing the back of it in front of you, you form a shield, physically protecting yourself. This suggests you're vulnerable and in need of protection. By turning the chair backwards however, you've literally turned convention around and appear a little too sure of yourself. Hiding behind this formidable barrier will make you feel more confident, but it's at a cost.

● **The chair grasp** As Desmond Morris says, this pose is the most obvious of all intention movements – any seemingly insignificant action which hints at what we're about to do next. Look at the hands braced on the side of the chair and bottom slightly raised – it's clear this man wants to get up but something is stopping him. The locked ankles under the chair also hint at his frustration; he's literally holding himself back.

how not to sit

"Sitting like this says 'Come and talk to me'"

Compare how you sit in a job interview with your sprawled self slouched on the sofa watching late-night telly and you don't need me to tell you the way we sit sends strong signals to others. Everything from the angle of our bottom on a bar stool to how, when, and why we cross our legs tells a story.

Exposing wrist and palm The head turn and direct gaze are definite green lights to spark up conversation. One hand lifted to the neck, exposes the wrist and palm, showing honesty and a willingness to share intimacy.

The top leg cross The way a woman's top leg is crossed is crucial. Crossed towards you, it's good news. Here, they're crossed away but a simple turn of her body on approach will fix it.

Hand on her thigh She's drawing attention to her legs, inviting you to admire them. Women are ten times more likely to clasp their thigh than men are. By placing her hand there she's imitating a lover's touch.

Straight but relaxed back Sitting erect means she's squaring – trying to make her body look as attractive as possible. A slight bend to the spine stops the pose looking too uptight.

how to sit

making an entrance

The no-fail way to make a fab first impression

- **Prepare mentally** Even if people don't turn their heads or avert their eyes, everyone notices a new arrival. It doesn't mean you're doing something wrong if people stare. Mentally steel yourself for the attention, by imagining your best friend is inside the room waiting for you.

- **Prepare physically** Pull shoulders back and down, adjust your clothing if it needs it, remember to breathe, smooth your forehead, uncurl your hands, unfold everything, relax your mouth.

- **Pause in the doorway** Every fibre of your self-conscious being will tell you to race inside and flatten yourself against the nearest wall. Don't. Stand naturally in the doorway – arms loosely by your side, head up, with relaxed posture and a half smile on your face – for a count of *one, two, three* and half the battle is won. People will automatically assume you're confident.

- **Make eye contact** Smile and look at the people closest to you. If they don't respond, shift your gaze so it looks like you were smiling at someone behind them. (They'll then feel like the idiot, rather than you!)

"Hold your drink high and you appear defensive. Keep it at waist height or lower"

- **Walk inside** Cut a path straight through the centre of the room. Walk with a purpose – even if you head for the bathroom – and you'll seem self-assured. Start by finding the host or someone who is the reason for you being there. Have a few prepared questions to kick off that conversation.
- **Ask to be introduced to people** Say hello with energy. Smile broadly and your voice will automatically sound friendly.
- **Shake hands** – it's not too formal, it looks classy plus it gives you a chance to touch. (Make it memorable by turning to pp.36-37.)
- **Make direct eye contact** Do this while saying hello and repeating their name. Lock eyes, count to three, then break it. Repeat their name three times: once when you meet, once during conversation, once when you say goodbye.
- **Don't fidget and fiddle** Excessive fiddling with clothes or hair will make you seem obsessed with your appearance. Fiddling with anything is usually a giveaway you feel nervous.

Do first impressions really stick?

Psychologists showed college professors, teachers, and students 30-second clips of individuals they would meet that semester. They were then asked to predict how well the person would perform and how they would feel about them at the end of term. Several months later, having got to know the person, they rated them again. Surprise, surprise (not), their predictions were astonishingly accurate. Later studies showing 15 seconds and then just six seconds of film produced remarkably successful predictions. Body language, clothes, posture, speech patterns – all give us away pretty much instantly. How is yours?

1

how close to stand

2

Moving in

Proxemics is the study of human spatial zones – the space we need to feel comfortable. Stand too close and you'll be branded too forward, pushy or downright sleazy. Stand too far away and you'll be seen as cold, distant, and hard to get to know. The perfect distance? Read on…

1

The personal zone (45–122 cm)
Strangers who've been chatting for a while stand this distance apart. If someone stands closer or farther away than normal, find out where they live. People from densely populated countries are used to less personal space and stand closer, as do city dwellers.

2

The intimate zone (15–45 cm)
This zone is for friends and lovers, so if a stranger – one we don't want to get to know better – comes this close, our involuntary response is to take a step backward to maintain the previous distance. If you'd like to make it clear you want more but aren't sure how the person you're with feels, move into the intimate zone after you've been chatting animatedly for around half an hour to an hour. If the other person doesn't step or lean back, your advances are probably welcome.

"Stand close, but leave space to flirt"

3

The close intimate zone (0–15 cm)

People only come this close for a reason – to attack, to whisper, or to kiss us. Assuming you're after the latter, gauge their response by leaning forward lots, while keeping your feet back in the intimate zone. Then touch in a safe place (lower arm or hand). If they don't withdraw, but instead lean toward you, you're safe to slide into the snuggle zone.

3

If in doubt, smile!
Smiling is truly contagious and it's a quick, subtle way to show interest without looking desperate

The three most common smiles are:

1. The simple smile What we do when smiling to ourselves. We don't expose any teeth, our lips simply curve upward. It's also the right smile to use to signal sexual interest. A broad smile removes all mystery, making "the chase" redundant and you appear friendly rather than flirty. This is not a good thing!

2. The upper smile The smile we give to friends. The mouth curves and the lips peel back to expose the upper teeth. Often, it's accompanied by a rapid flash of the eyebrows (a swift lift and lower) and eye contact. Use it to dazzle once you're chatting to your prey.

3. The broad or open smile Now the lips draw back to show both upper and lower teeth and our mouth opens wider. This is the smile that precedes or follows laughter. Interestingly, while this is the "merriest" and most playful of the smiles, people make little or no eye contact during it.

how to smile

"The best
smile to
flash if
you fancy
someone?
Slow and
secretive
is sexiest"

Are they fascinated – or falling asleep? Intent interest and utter boredom share similar signals. Spot the difference

Read the signs accurately and you'll know whether to end that fascinating story of your mother's trip to Greece or embellish it with your grandmother's adventures as well. The trick is to look for evaluation gestures, things we do when pensive and thoughtful. The classic gesture is fingers closed and resting on the cheek, with the index finger pointing upward toward the brain (which is, after all, the main organ used to process information). Spot someone doing this and they're still with you and thinking about the information you've given them. Watch carefully, though. A mere change in finger position can mean their mood has completely altered…

paying attention

● **Critical evaluation** Hand-to-cheek gestures – like the cheek resting on hand, body leaning forward – mean someone is deep in thought. If they're leaning *back* and assuming the pose illustrated left, however, the news isn't so good. They're attentive and thinking all right, but the index finger pointing vertically up the cheek and other fingers and the thumb positioned below the mouth and on the chin mean their thoughts may be negative and critical. Also look to see if the fingers are resting on their face or literally holding their head up. The more the hand supports the chin, the more bored the person is.

- **Chin stroking** Here we see a female version of chin stroking. Both sexes do it as the non-verbal equivalent of "Hmm, let's see". If it's a particularly difficult problem they're pondering, they may also narrow their eyes. This person is about to make a decision. Watch their body language immediately after the chin stroking finishes to see what it will be. If they move into negative body language (crossing anything, leaning back, frowning), the answer is probably no. If they lean forward with an alert expression and remain "open" – arms and feet remain uncrossed – the answer is probably yes.

- **Glasses in the mouth** If the girl had tipped her chin down, looked up through lowered lashes and let us see her tongue, this gesture would be a direct come-on with a not-so-subtle reference to oral pleasures. With eyes turned away, mouth closed and head tilted, it means she is stalling for time. Sucking on the end of our glasses is a procrastination gesture which also makes it difficult to talk – by doing it, we're subconsciously forcing ourselves to listen more carefully. It's the equivalent of zipping up our lips.

paying attention

"You aren't going to **get anywhere** unless you get the basics right"

Tracey's Top Tips

Do your homework

Now, I bet a few of you have got this far and thought, "Excuse me, but isn't this meant to be a book about getting and being a great date?" Yes, it is. But to be brilliant at anything, you need to do your homework. The idea of Chapter One is to make sure your overall body language is free from fatal errors. Stand, sit, and walk in front of a mirror to check you're sending out the right signals, then study others to see if you can spot essential clues to their character – which, of course, are the keys to getting their attention. (Pick the sexiest people in the room and it shouldn't feel too much like homework!) While you're at it, keep the following in mind:

Sex it up

Turn a good walk into a great one: tuck your bottom under, push your hips forward, exaggerate the swing of your hips (yes, even if you're a guy!) and take long, confident strides forward. Think panther.

Get a boob job

Forget surgery. Push your shoulders back, stand tall, then tuck your elbows into your waist, letting the lower part of your arm stick out at the sides. It makes your breasts look larger and waist smaller. To complete the pose, put one leg forward.

Fake it

If you're too shy to look people in the eye, focus on the tip of their nose or the centre of their forehead. The person you're looking at won't notice but it feels much less intense your end. Once you're feeling more comfortable, move your eyes to make direct eye contact, but keep it to short bursts, returning to the "comfort zones" for a breather whenever it feels uncomfortable. It's also a great way to get yourself through periods when you feel put on the spot or the (temporarily unwelcome) centre of attention.

Make it

If you really want to impress, perform a full-body pivot when someone you adore walks in. Instead of turning side-on (half-hearted) to greet them, literally turn on your heel and pivot your body one hundred per cent, arms outstretched to hug them, an enormous grin on your face.

2

themeeting

her eye scan

Sizing each other up:
the power of a glance

Love at first sight might not be reliable or even long-lasting but instant attraction isn't just a figment of a hopeful imagination. Simply lock eyes with someone you're enormously attracted to and your heart rate quickens and blood pressure soars. We communicate more with our eyes than any other body part. Hide your eyes and you hide your emotions. Narrowed eyes scream suspicion, a raised brow poses a question, eyes brimming with tears radiate excitement or sorrow – our eyes and the muscles around them clearly communicate what emotion we're feeling. Which is why it's almost impossible to flirt or fall in love without eye contact – zero eye communication usually means zero connection. Just in case it isn't sinking in, let me put this even more clearly: if you want to pull a partner, it's crucial you get this bit right! Spend time studying the following sequence – particularly if you're a guy. It really helps you sort out who wants you and who doesn't!

Count the looks Interested men and women usually send three sidelong glances. The first from men starts at the feet and moves up the body to the face – scanning in order of what they think is important! Women start at the eyes and then look down, the order of what's most important to them. The first look we get

"Men scan from the feet up. **Women scan from the face down"**

is to see if we're worth looking at. You'll get a second look if they liked what they saw (to confirm the first), and a third if they're so impressed they're considering talking to you.

The four-second scan Pass this test and they'll keep glancing your way to evaluate how open you are to being approached. We look at strangers or uninteresting people for three seconds or less. If someone's tossing you continual four-second gazes, it's a definite sign they're keen.

How they break the gaze Now listen up, this is the interesting bit… how a woman breaks eye contact is critical. If she moves her eyes to the side, continuing to look around the room, hailing a cab won't be necessary. She's still searching for better. If her eyes drop straight to the floor before looking back up again to meet yours within 30 seconds to a minute, you've hit gold. Downcast eyes followed by a preening gesture or hair-tossing and she definitely likes what she sees. So far, so good!

his eye scan

A handshake is often the first touch. Touch bypasses the brain, giving a good "gut" impression

● **A fingertip grab** People associate a wimpy, weak grip like this with an equally pallid personality. Which can be true – grabbing fingers instead of a palm keeps the other person at a distance. If a woman shakes a man's hand like this, she's probably girly, traditional, and secretly considers men the superior sex. If a man shakes a woman's hand this way, it could mean the same – or that he's madly attracted and terrified to let her get closer!

● **The knuckle crusher** A handshake is a modification of the primitive gesture of raising both hands to show you aren't holding any weapons. Shaking so hard you hurt means quite the opposite – you're ready to do battle. Very often, the knuckle crusher's hand is attached to a stiff-arm – again, designed to keep you at a distance. A person who shakes hands this way needs serious winning over. Are you sure it's worth the effort?

how to shake hands

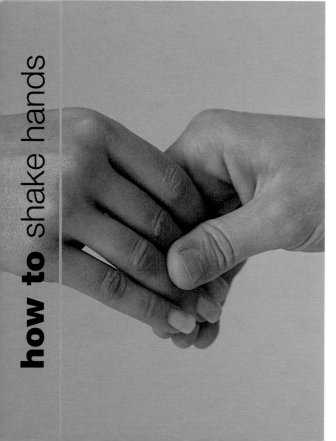

● **The sandwich** Holding someone's hand in both of yours, like a glove, can be the best thing you ever did – or social suicide. Used on someone you've just met, it'll probably be seen as smarmy and suspicious (hence it's nickname "the politician's handshake" – *how do you know you like me, you don't know me?*). Use it as a goodbye with someone you've been chatting to intensely, however, and it's ultra-effective. It's meant to show sincerity and strong feeling. Make it even more special by maintaining eye contact, leaning forward, and moving close.

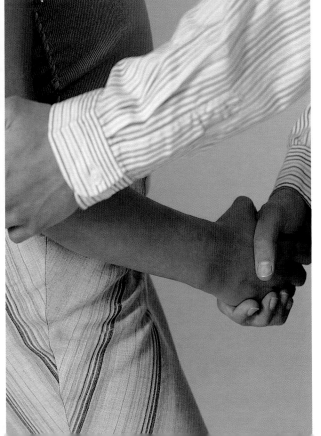

● **Elbow grab** Again, this can be a bit fake – think an over-eager, nervous host, keen for people to have a good time. But, given the right timing, killer eye contact, a smile, and an added little squeeze just before you let go and you've just let someone know you're wildly attracted to them, without anyone else knowing or having said a word! If someone looks away and giggles or laughs when you shake hands with them, it's a pretty safe bet they're embarrassed by the physical contact – which usually means they fancy you.

how to shake hands

How to spot who's single in a group – and make it clear you are

Most of us are mates with the opposite sex – without actually mating with them. How, then, do you know who's available and who's not when groups of friends go out? Initially, it's easy to confuse friendship and love. Things to watch for, whichever end you're on:

• **Where do they touch?** Women will happily sit on a friend's lap, but will almost never hold hands for long periods while sitting or standing. Theirs or their friend's hands also don't linger in sexual zones – they might playfully pinch a bottom but they won't stay there.

• **How close are they?** In-love couples tilt their heads toward each other. In-lust lovers, mesh the lower parts of their bodies.

• **What happens when they leave or return from the group?** Attached couples usually let the other know what they're up to, through a touch, a look, or words. When they talk, they'll look at their partner more than anyone else, glancing over frequently.

spot who's single

Last to leave?
Beware the closing effect

Studies of bar behaviour suggest the time a woman arrives at a bar – and certainly the time she leaves it – could dictate how much attention she'll get. In one study, a woman who rated 5/10 on the attractiveness scale at 7pm was rated 7/10 by 10.30pm and 8.5/10 at midnight. "Beer goggles" obviously enhanced the scores. Interestingly, women didn't alter their ratings over the time period regardless of how much they'd had to drink.

"The later the hour, the more attractive women look to unattached men"

A tempting trio
Three clear "come over" signs: a smile (I'm friendly); direct and inviting eye contact (I'm flirty); and head tilted on the side (I'm interested in you). Note also that she's put space between her and her friend.

Body turned toward you
Even if she weren't making direct eye contact, turning her torso your way is a subconscious sexual body display. Women do it to show off their breasts, men to show off their chest and shoulders. The top half usually turns first, starting with the shoulders.

Open formation
By pointing a foot toward you, she's saying you're welcome to join them and make it a threesome. Her body forms a 90-degree angle, effectively making a triangle with a gap left for you.

spot who's single

"One hand placed on a sexily cocked hip is often an invitation to join her"

time to **approach her**

He'll stand with hands on hips jacket pushed back, feet apart

- **A green light from her** Her shoulders are pulled back to thrust her breasts forward. (A good move – one study found a woman hitching could double the number of lifts she was offered by adding two inches of padding to her bra!) Putting a hand on the back of a hip emphasizes a tiny waist. Her eyes may also narrow – this sharpens focus and allows her to examine you more carefully. Not to mention making her look damn sexy!

- **A green light from him** He'll also perform a chest thrust to make himself look dominant. Both men and women swell and shrink accordingly to signal importance, fear, and desired attractiveness.

- **What they do with their coat** If they unbutton their jacket, it's a sign they're opening themselves up to meet people. Men stand with hands on both hips to ensure they take up lots of room and look bigger; women hold their arms close to their sides to achieve the opposite. If she leans forward and brings her arms in close to her body so the breasts press together and cleavage deepens, you really can turn back the bedsheets! Both sexes push their jackets back to signal body confidence: "Take a good look. You'll like what you see."

- **The double take** It's a natural reaction to seeing something delicious and unexpected – you look, turn away, then when the impact of what you've seen sinks in, turn back immediately. Dished up with a cheeky smile ("My God! How gorgeous are you!") it's dynamite! Shyer types can try locking eyes for a fraction of a second and looking straight to the floor, slightly embarrassed, before casting a swift glance over one shoulder.

time to **approach him**

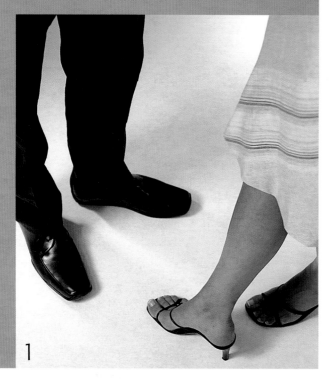

floor them

Read my
...feet

You can tell what's happening with this couple, just by looking at their feet. The transition from attracted strangers to flirtatious friends is clearly communicated purely through their feet position.

1

On target
His feet point squarely at his target, showing obvious (and, given he doesn't shift position, unwavering) interest. Initially she's not sure. One leg crosses over the other, meaning she's slightly defensive, but the front foot is angled to point in his direction, so it's still looking good.

2

Mirroring
She uncrosses her legs and moves closer, mirroring his feet position – a clear sign they're getting on well. Feet are an incredibly reliable indicator of our true feelings for one good reason: they're the body part farthest from the face. Few notice or think to control what our legs or feet are doing. This puts them extremely high on the believability scale. Walk into a meeting and you'll notice all feet usually point to the boss. Watch the feet of men at a party: their torsos might dutifully turn toward their partner but their feet will often point toward another pretty girl.

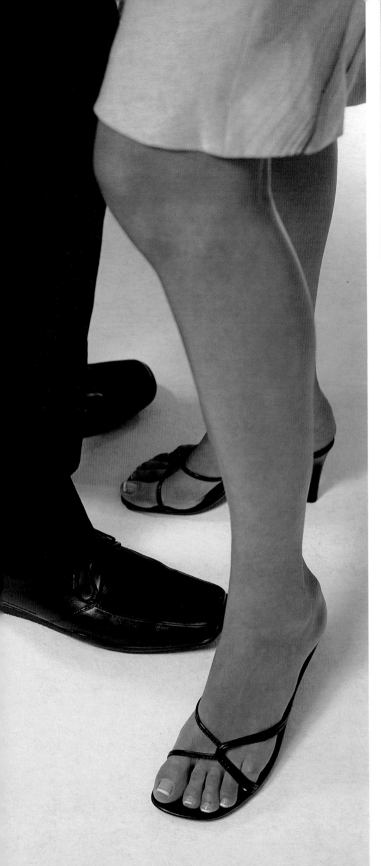

"We point with our feet **to what we want"**

3

Close up

The symbolism of her foot between his legs is obvious. Even better, the bent knee is almost touching his. Both suggest strong sexual interest. The icing on the cake would be if she kicked her shoes off when they sat down. Bare feet mean bed because taking your shoes off is the first stage of stripping. Our feet aren't the only things we point with, by the way. Both men and women put their hands on their hips, fingers splayed and pointing downward to show off another obvious good bit!

the **flirting** triangle

"We fall in love with large pupils without ever really knowing why"

- **The flirting triangle** When looking at strangers, we look from eye to eye, dipping slightly across the nose to make a tiny triangle. With friends, the triangle widens as eyes drop to include the nose and mouth. When looking at longed-for lovers, it broadens further to include even better bits like the breasts and genitals, hence the term "flirting triangle".

- **Pupil size** When lover's stare into each other's eyes, they're unconsciously checking the degree of pupil dilation. Bottomless, black pits instinctively reassure us all is well, pinprick pupils make us squirm for good reason – pupils enlarge when we like what we see. In one famous experiment, men were shown two pictures of an attractive girl, both identical except one set was doctored to make the pupils larger. Almost all judged the girl with bigger pupils more attractive, though none could say why. It almost certainly means that the men were attracted to the girl that they instinctively felt liked them. We like to be liked!

The first five seconds tell you everything

It's argued that the first five minutes when we meet someone is the most critical period. All impressions made after that will be measured against those initial decisions. Other experts – and I have to agree – say the first five seconds are the most telling. If you want to know if someone fancies you before they even know it themselves, watch for an eyebrow and face flash the minute your eyes lock. If they like what they see, their eyebrows will rise and fall, their nostrils and eyes will widen, and their lips part.

the **flirting** triangle

Women touch their throat
for different reasons: when they're feeling vulnerable or flirty

Not good (below): her hand winds around her throat or covers it (back of hand facing you) and stays in that position. You've offended her physically or emotionally and "gone for the jugular" – her hand flies into position literally to protect it by forming a barrier. The message to you is: stop whatever it is you're doing or talking about, backtrack and reassure her.

Good (opposite): stroking her throat, neck, or upper chest sends a definite erotic signal. Our throats and necks are "lovers-only" zones – no-one else gets to touch or kiss us there. If it's combined with a neck-arch, this signal is even more potent – by tilting her head to further expose her throat to your view she's hinting she's starting to trust you.

back off

"This stroking motion draws your eye **to her breasts"**

make a move

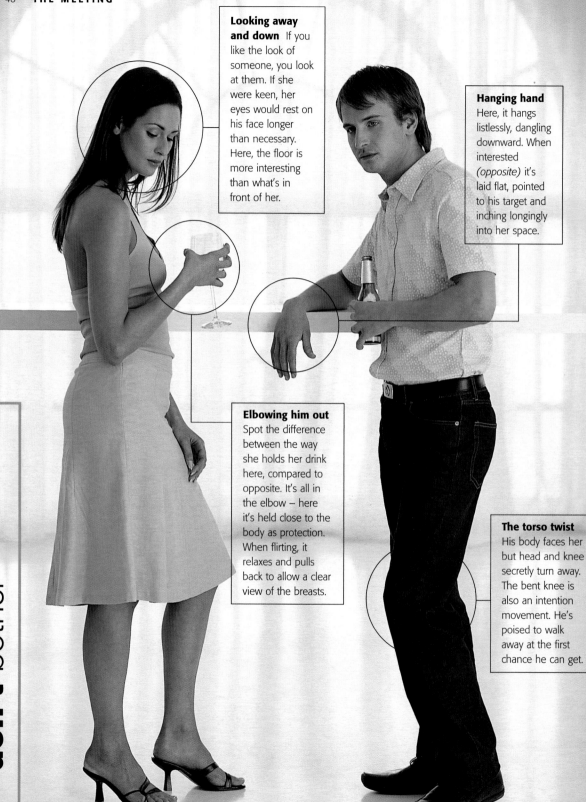

Looking away and down If you like the look of someone, you look at them. If she were keen, her eyes would rest on his face longer than necessary. Here, the floor is more interesting than what's in front of her.

Hanging hand Here, it hangs listlessly, dangling downward. When interested *(opposite)* it's laid flat, pointed to his target and inching longingly into her space.

Elbowing him out Spot the difference between the way she holds her drink here, compared to opposite. It's all in the elbow – here it's held close to the body as protection. When flirting, it relaxes and pulls back to allow a clear view of the breasts.

The torso twist His body faces her but head and knee secretly turn away. The bent knee is also an intention movement. He's poised to walk away at the first chance he can get.

don't bother

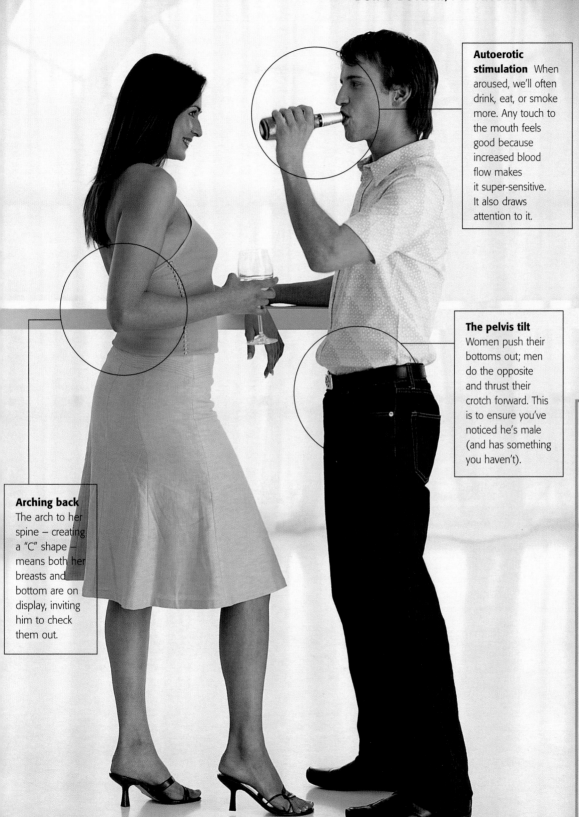

Autoerotic stimulation When aroused, we'll often drink, eat, or smoke more. Any touch to the mouth feels good because increased blood flow makes it super-sensitive. It also draws attention to it.

The pelvis tilt Women push their bottoms out; men do the opposite and thrust their crotch forward. This is to ensure you've noticed he's male (and has something you haven't).

Arching back The arch to her spine – creating a "C" shape – means both her breasts and bottom are on display, inviting him to check them out.

I'm **interested**

When vulnerable, our natural instinct is to hide behind a barrier. We feel safer behind a shield

● **Purse held as shield** As kids, we'd run and hide under Mum's skirts or beneath the nearest table when threatened. As adults, our instincts still tell us to do the same thing but, sadly, such behaviour is frowned upon. Instead, we erect more acceptable barriers: we'll place a chair or table in front of us or hold a purse, handbag, book, or drink high up, near to our chest, which gives us the illusion of safety.

● **Fiddling with shirt cuff** This is a disguised arm-cross – he's trying to conceal feeling uncertain. People who realize the implications of crossing their arms sneakily achieve the feeling of security through other means. An arm swings across the body but instead of gripping the other, the hand fiddles with a cufflink, bracelet, or pulls down a sleeve. Another disguised arm barrier? Holding a drink with both hands. It's not like we need two hands to hold a glass, is it now?

body blocks

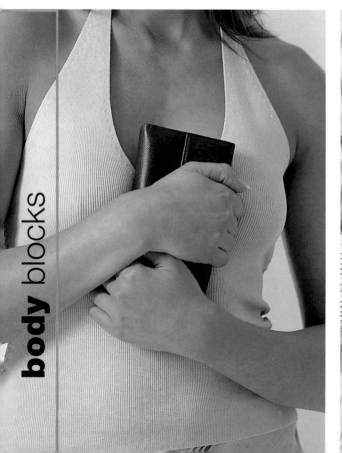

● **Partial arm barrier** Crossing arms tightly across the chest is an instinctive, primitive attempt to protect vital organs: the heart and lungs. It's also an obvious sign you're nervous or defensive. Holding one arm across the body is slightly more subtle and gets the same result, holding hands with yourself, in front of your body, is another version. Both sexes use arm barriers but women fold their arms much lower on the body. The reason? Breasts! As an alternative, try grounding yourself. You'll get the same comfort but look far more in control by lightly leaning against a wall or piece of furniture or by pressing the tips of your fingers against the edge of a table or chair for support.

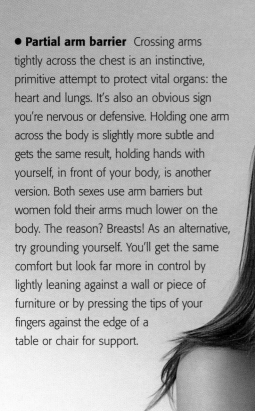

"Even one arm held **across the body** makes us look defensive"

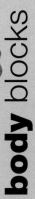

body blocks

"We can sense someone watching us even **with our backs turned**"

Tracey's Top Tips

Take the 60-second compatibility test

So little time, so many people to flirt with? If you can't decide who most deserves your attention, try this. Chat to someone for ten minutes, then answer the following questions, trying not to think too much about the answers: Would you like to kiss this person? Would they get on with your best friend? Would you like to have a child with this person? Would you like to be more like this person? Of course you don't have enough information to know the answers but your knee-jerk reaction will reveal more than you think.

Watch the way they fondle the furniture

Sometimes, we try to make contact through an intermediate object. The person who grabs hold of the back of the chair you're sitting on, or puts an arm along the back of the sofa behind you, is trying to get close. If they're sitting on a chair opposite you, they might lovingly caress the arms of it while looking longingly across at you. The message: they're too scared to touch you or they're testing to see what would happen if they did. If you don't lean away, it's OK to proceed.

See if they've sucked their tummy in

We let it all hang out when we're comfortable with people. When flirting, we do the opposite: stomach muscles tense as we desperately hold our tummies in. Too relaxed isn't good.

Don't make classic mistakes

Make too much eye contact and you'll be seen as superior, threatening, or adoring. Too little sends shy, insincere, or not-interested signals. Lowering your eyes briefly is a great flirting move but don't leave them down there or you'll be seen as submissive. If someone avoids looking at you, don't assume it always means lack of interest. You could be discussing a difficult subject or they might consider you of higher status than they are.

Do believe body language over words

If there's a choice, people will nearly always believe the body. "I hate you," said with a cheeky smile, tipped chin, and sexy smile actually means the opposite. "I don't fancy her" doesn't hold much weight if the person casts long, frequent glances at the girl in question.

thechat-up

3

What's the first thing you do when someone gorgeous walks in the room? Make sure you look your best of course!

It's called preening or grooming – "straightening ourselves out". Men smooth or ruffle their hair (depending on the style), straighten their tie, tweak their jackets, pull up sagging socks, and brush specks from their clothes. Women also check their hair with their hands, smooth skirts to show off their hips – and more often than not, disappear to the bathroom to do a full mirror check and lipstick touch-up. It's all part of the mating ritual. It's not until we think we look OK that we're ready to move into "illuminations" – me-Tarzan, you-Jane gestures that highlight the physical difference between the sexes. Sticking your breasts out, for instance, reminds him he doesn't have any. Standing with legs apart and crotch thrust forward does the same for her.

preening & grooming

Come here, go away – and why it works

It's called intermittent reinforcement. The most effective way to attract someone isn't to fall at their feet or to be frosty. Dole out affection infrequently. Say you meet at a party and initially flirt a lot. You'll get a drink and start chatting to someone else, looking over to smile occasionally. When you chat again, renew the flirting but less intensely. Given the mixed signals, they're now thinking, "Do they like me or not?" They'll work much harder than if you'd stuck by their side all evening.

"If they check or adjust their appearance **it is usually a big tick!"**

Smoothing an eyebrow Men send out far less flirting signals than women but a classic male preening sign is surreptitiously licking a finger and smoothing an unruly eyebrow into place.

Smoothing the thighs Women preen endlessly when in the company of someone stunning. The bottom half gets particular attention, probably because skirts and dresses often bunch up when we sit. Smoothing hands over thighs or hips is common.

preening & grooming

Guys, pay attention to her wrists and palms – they can tell you all you need to know

Women, almost predictably, flash their wrist at someone they're attracted to – it's such a clichéd feminine response that wrist-flashing often has a starring role in a drag queen's repertoire of exaggerated girly gestures. Watch while a woman fiddles with her hair, an earring, or smokes a cigarette, and look to see if the wrist is turned to face you, palm exposed. Great news if it is. Open palms nearly always mean good things – which is why a mere flick of the wrist can change the mood and message instantly. If the palms represent honesty and openness, the back of our hand says the opposite: bugger off. You'd prefer the creep coming way too close backed off big time? Copy the girl below – flip your hand, rest your chin on it, and you've effectively hung a neon sign saying "Bored"!

the twist of a wrist

Want to give the impression you know **exactly what you're talking about?**

Put your fingertips together, palms facing, and make a church steeple. It's called "steepling" (no, really) and it'll be the best thing you ever did with your fingers or the worst. It all rests on accompanying body language and how high your steeple is. If you're a bit of an authority on something, a high steeple is a good move – it shows you're confident and know your stuff. Tilt your head back and "look down your nose", however, and you'll transform into a pompous twit. The guy on the right is doing a "disguised steeple" with his index fingers, which also cover his mouth. He thinks he knows better than the person he's with and is trying to stop himself saying so. People tend to steeple up when talking and down (*bottom left*) when listening. We make a moderate steeple (*bottom right*) when we think we know more than the person speaking. Generally, the higher the steeple, the more arrogant you risk appearing. Which is why women (more fearful of looking arrogant than men) tend to favour the lowered variety.

superior steepling

"**Steepling could be** the best thing you ever did **with your fingers**"

legging it

Do the
legwork

We cross our arms instinctively to protect our heart and vital organs (and all the emotions associated with them), we cross our legs to shield our genitals (ditto). But while crossed arms nearly always have a negative connotation, women often cross their legs to show them off, to look "ladylike" or sexy. Because legs are in the bottom half of the body and farther away from our face and general vision, they're quite a reliable indicator of our true feelings.

Leg crossed high on thigh The higher she crosses her legs, the more sexual the signal and the more she fancies you. Add direct eye contact, a smile, and one hand leading your eyes to her genital area, and there's a *flashing* green light.

Open toe shoes Serious, sensible girls tend not to wear high, strappy sandals. If the shoes are frivolous – designed to look good, not good for comfort – she's more likely to be out for a fun time (and keen to meet you!).

"The more exposed thigh, the more likely it is she fancies him"

- **Sitting with legs apart** Confident men often sit this way but it's rare for a women to sit with legs apart, even if covered by jeans or trousers. In a skirt, she'd almost never assume this pose (unless you're already lovers and she's teasing you). Any woman who plants her legs wide open literally wears the pants. She's powerful and challenging. Not a good bet if you're looking for someone to bake cookies.

- **Sitting with legs tightly crossed** Men do it when they're feeling defensive. "Proper" girls do it to form an invisible chastity belt. Trouble is, the more fuss you make covering up your sexual parts, the more it draws other people's attention to them. Yanking down a too short skirt only highlights the length!

- **Walking on tiptoe** If she's on the beach, by a pool, or anywhere where women take their shoes off, whether or not she rises on her tiptoes is highly significant. If attractive men are around, she will. It makes legs look longer, bodies slimmer, and her look more feminine.

The show-off leg slide

Want to get noticed when sitting on a stool at the bar? If you're a girl, cross your legs high on the thigh, then lean down and grab the ankle of the top leg with the same side hand. Twist your hand so it's grabbing the outer side of your leg. Now let your hand slide up the calf and thigh, then when you get to the hips, bring the other hand in to slide both hands over your hips. Put your hands on the top of your thighs, lift your torso up and out of your hips, push your bottom out, and arch your back so your breasts stick out. Settle back, relax, and sip your drink. Do it in one, smooth motion and you'll hear jaws drop.

legging it

Sit like this if you
want to be ignored

No one likes being rejected and being greeted with an icy "Hi" (subscript: go away). When you've practically bounded across the room, tongue hanging out like an over-eager puppy, it's humiliating. Make sure that doesn't happen to you by correctly reading approachability signs – and only going on a green light.

Hand propping up the head This is just one of a cluster of signals that say this guy's not attracted to anyone in view. Instead of sitting straight to show off his body, he's slumped, his eyes roll to the ceiling (derision), and he's so bored, he can't even hold his head up without support.

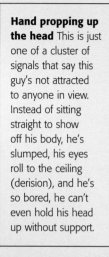

Leg kicking up and down If a girl does this, it's deliciously wicked – she's subconsciously thinking of sex and imitating thrusting. For men – and particularly given the accompanying signals – this leg jiggle means he's restless and frustrated.

red light

"A deliberate pose says **'I want attention'**"

Leaning sideways
The way we lean reveals whether we like someone or not. Quite logically, we lean toward people we like and away from people we don't like. She's leaning forward to show interest and also to the side. Sitting asymmetrically means she's relaxed.

Clasped hands Her hands are clasped in front of her, which could mean she's protective, but it's a loose grip. The real reason is she's holding her elbows close to her side to create a nice visual line. With legs swept so far to the side, she's also balancing herself.

Legs swung to the side She's deliberately arranged her legs in this position to make them look longer – an obvious attempt to "pose" and look good for whoever's watching. The more often she crosses and uncrosses her legs while facing her target, the better his chances.

green light

Stop and take stock: how to tell if you're doing OK and a reminder of why you're doing it

Just in case you were naughty and skipped the intro, let's remind ourselves what we're trying to do here. To qualify as a "superdate", you need to a) attract the person you want; b) seduce the person you want; c) make them fall in love with you. (Sorry about the order, but that's the reality of how it usually happens!) Most people accept there are a few underlying musts to this formula – few would argue looking healthy, dressing well, and being generally pleasant helps. But not too many people stop to think about their body language. Which is odd (not to mention rather stupid), when 55 per cent of the impression we have of someone is based on their body language.

This is a good point in the book to reiterate where all the information you've been reading ultimately came from. So far, you're (hopefully) faithfully pointing your toes, steepling fingers, and doing God

how's it going?

Mixed messages? Try this

Check their signals: take a step back to observe properly. *Check your signals:* look down. What's your body doing? *Count to four:* can you see at least four signs they like you? Wishful thinking makes us read too much into others' body language. *Change position:* if they mirror you, it's good news. *Leave briefly, then come back:* if they're in the same place, they were hoping you'd return to them.

"Check your volume control. Are you too obvious, or too subtle?"

knows what else. But it's around this point that it all starts to get a bit hard and people think: "Ummm….exactly why am I doing all this again? Like, how did zoologists and body language experts come up with all this seeming nonsense about keeping your palms up, wrists flashed, and chin dipped?"

Well, by studying animals and humans and watching how both act in, and react to, different situations. From there, they're able to piece together common body language gestures for different moods (happy, hostile) and personality types (introvert, confident). If all the confident people they studied, stood with their right finger in their ear, that gesture then goes on the "confident person" list. (Tell me you know I'm joking about the finger in the ear!)

Now, this is how it works to help you: if you stand, sit, walk, and generally do whatever other confident/sexy/attractive/successful/popular people do, people will think you are also confident (sexy, etc.) because that's what's proved true in the past. You'll also find that as you adopt the gestures of a confident person, others around will react to you differently, which in turn will give you greater confidence. So even if some of this advice does sound a bit weird and you aren't really sure why putting your thumbs on display is going to get you laid, trust me. Hang in there. This is a quick, visual reference book so I've spared you lots of the theory but all the tips are tried and tested and come from reputable sources.

"Never judge on one thing alone. Look for consistent messages"

How to tell if they want more

Test their intentions by doing the following:

Step in, then back While you're chatting, take a step forward into the space between you, then quickly step back again. This draws attention to the space between you. If they're keen, they'll now step forward to close the gap without really knowing why.

Drop your voice so it's almost a whisper If they stand where they are, cup their ear, and shout "I can't hear you? Can you speak up?", they aren't interested in getting close.

how's it going?

He can't

Touch is vital but when, where, and how is critical. Because men are more sex driven than women, and women have more body parts with sexual connotations (breasts, thighs, bottom), men need to avoid any erotic zone, or risk being branded "he's only after me for sex".

She can

Because women tend to be driven by romance, touches on his personal parts (bar *that* part) are seen as innocent. She can place a hand on his chest, to show she shares his feelings, or even his thigh – though the closer your hand is to the genitals, the more likely it is to be taken as a come-on.

how to touch

No-go zones

Men are physically stronger than women. Which means any of his gestures that involve touching taboo areas, coming too close, or gripping can feel threatening. It also pays to keep it soft and light. We touch the way we like to be touched and men's skin is tougher, meaning their touch is harder.

Much better

By stepping back, loosening the grip, and adding an "I won't harm you" smile, the first gesture will now be received as it was intended: to show reassurance, rather than inspire fear. By moving his hand from top of the bottom to middle of the back in the second, he's now guiding rather than fondling.

how to touch

Some body language looks so bad, it's obviously not a good idea. But seemingly insignificant things can often make or break

Simply avoiding things like tightly folded arms, won't keep you out of trouble. More subtle actions – like those opposite – will also strongly influence who's still hanging around when you come back from getting a drink – and who hot-footed it the second your back was turned. Some of our less lovable habits are called displacement activities: small, trivial, repetitive, fidgety things we do when under stress. I'm talking drumming fingers, tapping feet, jiggling legs, clicking pens, shredding napkins, doodling, checking and rechecking schedules, and the dozens of other movements people make when under stress that annoy the hell out of everyone else. If people seem agitated, uncomfortable, or don't seem to relax around you, watch for any constant fiddles and fidgets. This will probably be why.

innocent but off-putting

The body
rarely lies

Pretend all you like that you're not interested in the new head of marketing – others say he's sex-on-legs but you haven't noticed (yeah right!) – but you'll still tug or twist at your wedding ring each time he chats to you. Why? You might kid yourself you aren't affected by his charms but your body's not quite as coy. We often play with any ring signifying commitment when we talk to someone who's simultaneously forbidden and gorgeous. It subconsciously rids us of commitment for that stolen period. Naughty? Yes. But it's not really your fault if it's automatic, is it now?

"Under pressure our bodies leak. Our true feelings come gushing out in gestures"

"Subtle signals like this can **put them off**"

Arm clasped behind back. It's a "get hold of yourself" gesture. Men, particularly, stand this way if it's crucial to maintain self-control. Look around any formal event and you'll see plenty of examples.

Rocking on heels
Mothers rock babies to soothe them, most instinctively rocking at the same speed as the heartbeat heard in the womb. As adults, we recreate this security by rocking on our heels.

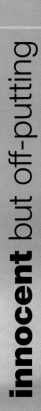

innocent but off-putting

Check out the way they're standing for insider info

- **Straddled, feet wide apart** The guy who stands with feet apart has a flashing sign above his head saying "Pick me if you want a real man". Dominant men stand like this because it widens their body and makes them take up lots of space. Usually the crotch area is thrust forward, highlighting the other part he's rather proud of! The good news (or bad, depending on how you like your men) is that this guy's settled in for a while.

- **Legs loosely crossed at calves, arms crossed low and loose** Look at a group of strangers and this is probably what you'll see. It's a protective, defensive standing position but it's not hostile. This person is just nervous and uncomfortable – less flirting, more friendly reassuring chat.

- **Legs crossed like blades of scissors** A favourite for both men and women who are submissive and shy. They're all yours to bring out of their shell though – the leg position means they couldn't leave quickly even if they wanted to.

"How they stand tells you how much they want to stay"

- **The busy bee** People with places to be, people to see, stand with weight on one hip, the foot of the straight leg pointed toward the person, the foot of the bent leg pointing away. This person wants to leave – they're walking on the spot.

- **Heels snapped together** This guy's hedging his bets – they don't want to stay but they don't want to go. Non-committal – up the flirting factor and see what happens next!

There are two other signs worth watching for, which seem to be peculiar to men chatting up women. The first: an isolation attempt. If he's interested, his instinct will be to separate you from the group (your friends, his friends, any other men hanging around) in the hope of getting your full attention. Also steal a quick look at his chest. If he's doing some chest puffing, he's trying hard to appeal subliminally by looking strong. (Women do the same thing, by the way, for the same reason – except we're highlighting the male/female breast difference.)

stand up to them

To pout or not to pout?

Marilyn Monroe mastered it, the rest of us can end up looking like a rather sad extra in a porn film. But lasciviously licking the lips and pouting both draw attention to the mouth, home of many sexual pleasures. It also highlights the fact that a female's lips are more luscious than a man's. When aroused, female lips (both kinds) become swollen and redder in colour – hence why a pout and lipstick are seen as sexy. Pouting makes lips seem fuller; it also explains why bright red lipstick is seen as so blatantly sexy, it's brash.

I spy... a party animal

When we do things we shouldn't, our body often finds a way to tell us something is wrong. An eye twitch is a muscle contraction or spasm usually brought on by tension or stress (too much work, drinking, smoking, partying, etc.) If it's you twitching away, ease up and get some sleep. If it's the person chatting you up, they might be the party animal – or be feeling under pressure. Ditto the person who is blinking excessively – they're nervous or insecure.

Our eyes can respond to one and a half million simultaneous messages – hardly surprising, then, that we use them to communicate more than any other part of our body. This is one reason why big eyes are a plus – the signals are clearer. Make yours look huge by doing what Princess Di did whenever a camera pointed her way: dip your chin so the top of your face, including your eyes, seems bigger. You can also try:

- **An eye flash** If a man is looking at her and their eyes lock, women will often raise their upper eyelids slightly and rapidly. It's a subtle eye-opening movement which says "Yes, it's definitely you I'm looking at".
- **Can't take my eyes off you** When we're attracted, we really do have difficulty dragging our eyes away. The person stops talking, someone else starts – and we're still gazing adoringly even though they're silent. Do it deliberately for startling effect. Keep your eyes on theirs for a slow count of five during the silence that follows after you, or they, stop talking.
- **Fake "bedroom eyes"** They're essentially eyes with big pupils (they dilate when they like what they see) and lots of moisture (tears pool when we're excited by someone). Get the look by holding your eyes open extra-wide, trying not to blink until tears form, then shutting them for a few seconds to block out light (another way to alter pupil size). When you reopen, voilà! Shiny eyes with lots of pupil action!

"Dip
your chin
**and do
a Di"**

Around fifty-five per cent of us "see" the world, fifteen per cent "hear" it, and thirty per cent "feel" it

How we filter the constant stream of information we receive about the world depends on which of our senses is the most dominant. You might both be in the same restaurant on a first date, but what you're experiencing could be dramatically different. Visuals are looking at the décor, what everyone's wearing, and admiring the food presentation. Auditory people are busy eavesdropping, listening to the background music, and reading the menu out loud. Kinesthetics (or kino's) feel the world, so are driven by physical sensation. They're the ones touching the tablecloth, drinking in the atmosphere, and trying to analyse your emotions. When we "click" with someone it usually means they're the same type – they've travelled through the world taking the same journey.

sense your type

"Looking for your soulmate? Search for someone who's the same sensory type as you – they experience the world the same way"

Who's who?

We all experience the world through sight, sound, and feelings so most of us are a mix of all three types. But post childhood, nearly all of us have one sense that is our favourite and becomes dominant. It's in your interest to know which type your lusted-after love object prefers, because you know how they relate to the work, you can communicate to them on their wavelength. When you match yourself up with another person's favourite sense, you're not only talking the same language, but seeing through the same eyes, hearing through the same ears, and feeling the same feelings. How could they *not* be seduced by you?

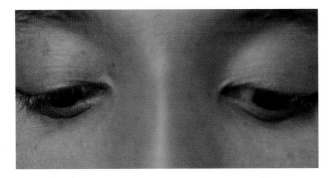

1

Eyes down = kinesthetic They look to their hearts. Not surprisingly, they're big touchers, often physical, and (bonus!) highly sexed.
Tips: Buy presents with textures that feel nice to stroke, talk slowly – it takes longer to feel words than see or hear them.

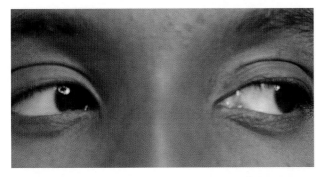

2

Eyes to the side = auditory
They look to their ears. Things need to sound good to get their attention. They've got great voices and often work with words and sounds in music or broadcasting.
Tips: Take them to concerts, leave voicemail rather than text, and instigate long chats.

3

Eyes up = visuals
They look to their imaginations. Because they "see" the world, visuals care a lot about how things look. They talk fast and move their hands a lot, drawing pictures with words.
Tips: Look good, take them pretty places, and use phrases like "I see".

sense your type

Naughty thoughts lead to auto-erotic touching –
subconsciously touching ourselves for three (very good) reasons

The first is to draw attention to a body part we'd like the other person to notice – the reason why females slide hands over thighs, waists, hips, and upper arms, and both sexes stroke their lips with their fingers (sometimes even slipping one sexily inside the mouth). We also touch ourselves to tease – "Wouldn't you like me to be touching you like this? Or you touching me?" Finally, we touch because it feels good. When we're sexually excited, blood rushes to our extremities (not just that one!), engorging the lips and making them feel supersensitive. If someone starts drinking or eating faster when you flirt with them, it's having the right effect.

secret signals

"Think sex and you'll probably touch your mouth"

If we'd like to sleep with someone, we often instinctively kiss, lick, or caress objects…

Especially those that subconsciously remind us of sex. Watch for men stroking their ties (some say an arrow pointing to the penis), fiddling with change in their pocket (the closest he can get to a quick fiddle without getting arrested), sliding rings up and down a finger (imitating thrusting), or rubbing their nose (a phallic symbol). Women suck pens and fingers (pretend penises), lick ice-creams, and let spoons slide sensually out of their mouth (pretend oral sex). Yes, sometimes it's unintentional and meaningless, but combined with other positive signs, pseudo-sexual signals count. Particularly watch if they start playing with their wine glass. Women slide fingers up and down the stem, men tend to circle the rim with their finger – cleverly reflecting the different way we touch respective body parts!

touch and tease

She'll use her hair to show she's keen

Once a woman's got your attention, she'll signal availability by either running her fingers through her hair, fluffing it, or (best of all) doing a head toss so it flicks and bounces around. It's designed to show how healthy (and therefore young) her hair (and she) is. One of the few times an uninterested female will touch her hair is to pull long hair out from behind her ear, to let it fall in a curtain, stopping you watching her face. Not good. Give up now.

"Sticking something in your mouth can mean you're up for it"

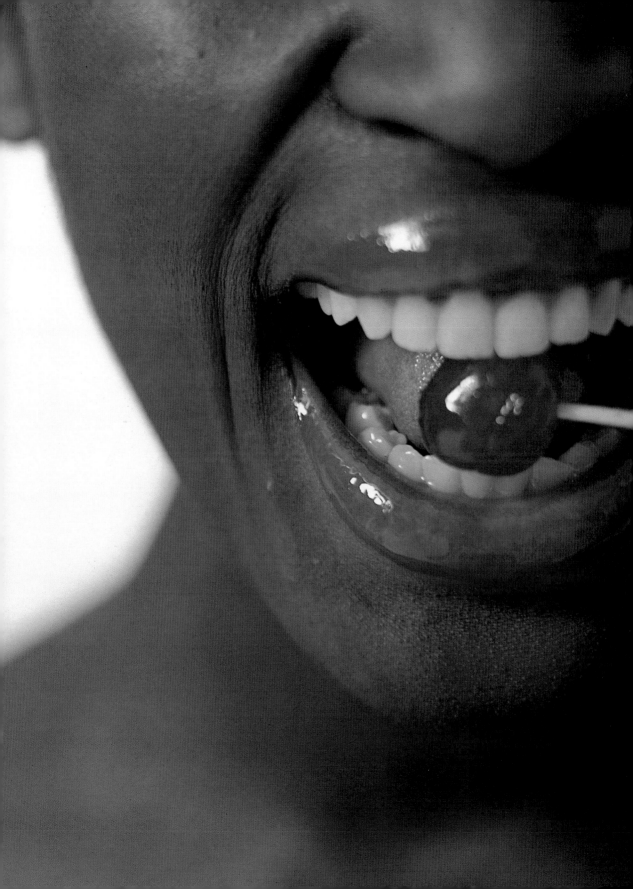

Want their attention? Whisper to the person next to you

Sounds odd, works like magic! Make direct eye contact with them, give a little smile, then whisper into the ear of the person you're with. It doesn't matter what you say – they'll still think you're talking about them and curiosity drives most of us nuts. Even if they're shy, they'll keep stealing glances in your direction. If they're confident, they'll find a way to stand close, raising a quizzical eyebrow. The brave will come straight up and ask what you said. Whispers make us think someone is saying something awfully nice or awfully horrible about us – why else would they whisper it? Either way, it gets the adrenalin pumping and them looking your way. (Pretty easy from there to convince them it's complimentary!) Whispers also work when you're already chatting to the person. Once you've both warmed up, lean forward, and whisper into their ear. It could be conspiratorial ("I don't know about you, but I'm not convinced about that painting") or a compliment ("You're very funny by the way"). Then simply pull back, smile, and continue the conversation. Be warned though: this shifts gears rather rapidly and most men will interpret it as a signal for them to put their foot heavy on the flirting accelerator.

sneaky tricks

"Mix up their stuff. Plonk your coat on top of theirs. Do they look pleased or panicked to see their things muddled with yours?"

Reel them in: more devious ploys to grab their attention

Make up a (flattering) nickname It makes them feel special – you've noticed something unusual about them. It also instantly puts things on a more personal level, the same effect as remembering to mention their name.

Ask for a headache pill If he's out to impress, he'll search high and low to find you one, then has the perfect excuse to hang around and look after you. If you're really cheeky, ask him to massage your hands or head – it really does help ease tension and creates a nice little excuse for some sensual touching.

Ask for a light If they hand you a lighter, they're shy, not interested or seeing someone else. If they do offer to light your cigarette for you and lean in, up the intensity by making direct eye contact as the flame connects.

Sit next to them Even better if you can make a bit of fuss to do so. (Do it in a friendly way and you won't look desperate.) Do they look pleased? Snuggle in? Or move their body or an object to create distance between you? Moving elsewhere should be obvious (i.e the "then he-said, then I said" phonecall won't be necessary later that night.)

Play mum Everyone likes being taken care of – particularly if the person coming to their aid happens to be captivatingly sexy! Notice when people need things (a fresh drink, fresh air, a jacket, the time…)

Play it personal If you want to move things beyond boring chit-chat, volunteer something personal about yourself. The more you open up, the more likely they are to follow.

Be happy Unless you've got the self-deprecating humour routine down pat, few of us get away with being constantly grumpy. Who would you rather hang around with? A depressed, unhappy moaner or a funny optimistic, who makes life seem bright and full of promise?

The giveaway sign they fancy you

Glance over your shoulder when you visit the bathroom during those first few meetings and it's almost guaranteed you'll know if they're sexually interested or not. If you see them checking out your bottom, it's nearly always a yes – for both sexes. Peer around the corner to see what they do next: after you've disappear from sight, their next move is usually to check their hair is behaving.

sneaky tricks

Body language is both primitive and logical. If someone's pushing the right buttons, it tries very hard to get us naked with that person

This is why we remove jackets, undo buttons, loosen ties, and push up our sleeves – we're symbolically stripping. It's the polite, public version of slipping into something "more comfortable" (easily removable) and it sends LOUD sexual signals. A woman who lets a strap fall off her shoulder – and leaves it there – is saying "Look, I'm getting undressed already". Leaving a shoulder exposed allows him to imagine she is already topless. Semi-clothed is often sexier than completely naked, which is why both sexes wear "peekaboo" clothes – ripped jeans or tops and (for her) skirts with splits – all serving up a tantalising glimpse of flesh.

symbolic stripping

Lighten up
the mood

You think they're sex-on-legs but the
cloud hovering above them means you
don't stand a chance – or do you?
To change someone's mood or mind,
simply change their position.

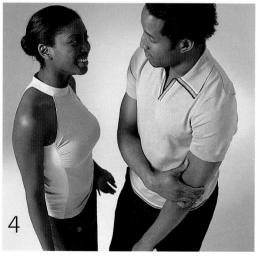

1

Mirror them This is the only time I'll get you to mirror bad body language! Cross whatever they've got crossed and stand the way they are to subliminally show you're on the same emotional level.

2

Unfold one arm Once you've warmed them up with words, subtly drop one arm. If, after a while, they haven't dropped one of theirs, cross both arms again, keep the conversation non-threatening, and smile, before trying again.

3

Wait for them to follow If they're trusting you, they'll start to physically/emotionally open up. Even if arms are crossed but loosened, it's a start. If nothing's happening, hand them something to force them to break the hold.

4

Drop both arms You've now led by example and shifted your posture from closed to open, one step at a time. Be patient at this point. Dropping their second arm – the final barrier between you – is maybe a bit scary!

5

Don't make any sudden moves They've now completely exposed themselves (so to speak) but now's not the time for big gestures like moving too close or touching. Stay friendly but not flirty for at least 10 minutes (and that does mean not so much as a hair-flick!).

"I'm not feeling defensive or nervous, it just feels comfortable." People who claim this are partly right – crossing your arms does feel comfy., but only because it's the body language matching the feelings. Even if it feels right, don't do it!

"Come hither" lips and look The moist, slightly parted lips subliminally suggest other parts of her may look the same. Combine this sexual mimicking with a revealing dress in a bright colour and most men would lay bets she's broadcasting sexual availability. Why else would she wear such an attention-getting dress? What's more likely is that she's attracting the attention of the bunch, with the hope of finding one mate.

Cover up, get away with more

Dress "sexily" – anything plunging, curve-clinging or thigh skimming for her; tight, chest-revealing or suspiciously thought-about for him – and people will assume you're on the pull. Which you probably are! But you should still be aware that what you're wearing will influence the flirting moves you use.

sex kitten

Bare thighs Exposing the upper thigh so deliberately says "Come here big boy" clearer than any words could ever express.

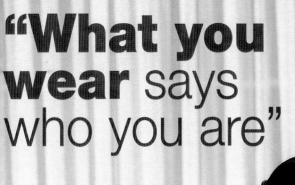

"What you wear says who you are"

High collar = class Despite her breasts being accentuated by the cut and cling of the sweater, any top that goes higher than the neckline sends schoolmarmish signals. Feel free to pull out all the stops – the most over-the-top flirting moves are fine when dressed so conservatively.

The demure arm The postures here are virtual mirror images – except for a subtle change in arm position. By lifting the arm up and placing it along one thigh, she's covered up her breasts. Holding it back and away from the body *(left)* is bolder since it invites admiring eyes to take a good, uninterrupted look at her body.

subtle sexy

"Take a few risks, and see what happens"

Tracey's Top Tips

Leave a lasting impression

Don't ruin a great entrance by blowing it on departure and making a fuss about leaving. Insist on saying loud goodbyes to everyone and you'll look insecure and desperate to be included next time (Don't forget me!). Unless you can discreetly say goodbye to the host/ess, do it the next day. Announcing you're going could give others the same idea. Whatever you do, don't look back when walking out. If people are watching you exit, they'll admire you even more if you don't glance back anxiously.

Colour people's perceptions

The colours we wear strongly affect people's perceptions of us. Dress a baby in black and you'd be reported to the social services; James Bond would look anything but debonair prancing about in a hot pink suit. The colour you wear and where you wear it are all highly significant. A siren red sweater worn under a suit to a business function suggests confidence and power, a red miniskirt worn to meet your partner's parents suggests stupidity.

Don't forget to move

Confident people change positions once every two or three minutes, altering their weight and moving subtly and smoothly into new postures. The trick is to think energetically without moving too rapidly or fidgeting. (Easier than it sounds!)

Sure you want to fall in love?

It's a known fact that single women travel more, are more likely to buy French perfume and sports cars, and look better for longer than their married sisters. For every seven pounds a married woman with a child puts on, an unmarried woman gains two pounds. The moral according to Desmond Morris: If you want to stay girl-shaped, retain girl-status!

It beats botox

Wage war on wrinkles the cheap, pain-free way: hang around someone adorable. When we look at someone we like, our faces relax, soften, and glow; harsh lines fade and we look younger. It works a treat long term too. When we're conscious of people watching our faces, we adjust our expressions to look "perky". But before long they soon fall into the facial position we assume most of the time. If you're mostly happy, that won't be a problem, will it?

the**date**

Most dates
end up at
dinner

Which means sitting opposite each other, separated only by a table. Women handle this well (coffees with girlfriends), shy men find it acutely embarrassing. It's face-to-face, so it's intimate and how are you supposed to sit? Don't be guilty of his classic mistakes.

Wall of hands
Tightly knitted fingers and thumbs against your mouth says "I'm nervous and don't know what to say".

Closed posture
The clenched hands, tense posture, and downward glance give the impression he's "folded in" – not open to her (or a relationship). Sadly, he's more likely to be nervous and unaware of the signals he's sending.

Feet aren't grounded We put both feet flat on the floor when we're on firm ground – sure of ourselves. Compare her confident feet position with his crossed ankles and tipped feet. He's feeling off-balance emotionally.

date flake

Direct gaze and animated face Everything about this girl's pose says "You have my full attention and I want to hear what you have to say". In action, you'd see that her blink rate is slow; the more anxious someone is, the more often they blink.

Leaning forward, knees together With a straight back and feet under her knees, she's sitting in a neutral "step" posture. If her knees were apart, she'd be signalling dominance. Together but not tightly pressed, they enforce her air of "you're on friendly territory".

Hands on table, palms up Anxious hands play with objects or hang onto each other for reassurance. Placing them on the table, uncrossed and palms upward, says "See? I have nothing to hide".

date diva

Modern lovers have it easy. **Today's "love letter" – the text or email** – is a lot less hassle than the old variety

If you think waiting for a phone call is bad, imagine lying around your castle, agonising does she/he like me, for days or weeks on end, before the mounted messenger finally arrived! Today's equivalent – text and emails – offer cheap, immediate communication. We're able to tell the person we lust after exactly how we feel, at the exact moment we feel it. Fabulous, eh? Or not…

Just about all of us have woken up after a heavy night and nearly passed out when our phone swims into view, looking suspiciously used. What felt right to send at 3am – drunk, emotional, and desperate for a cuddle (etc.) – suddenly seems completely inappropriate at 7am. And you can bet your next five headache pills, it was. The main plus of text and email – instant gratification – is also the main negative. Emotions like love, lust, anger, and jealousy can be fleeting but they're powerful and have a tendency to take over and hold other more sensible brain inhabitants – like logic and judgement – hostage.

hi-tech flirting

The blind email date

Flirting via email with someone you've never set eyes on is both irresistibly appealing and ridiculously stupid. Exactly the reason why we all do it! You start out being a bit playful with someone you deal with through work, next minute, there you are about to meet them for the first time and practically passing out with anticipation. Sometimes, it's lust at first look. More often, it's mutual and massive disappointment: what worked through words, doesn't cut it in the flesh. So pained, polite emails replace the previously frisky ones Go for it but be warned!

"Sign your name **the first time.** They may not have stored your **phone number**"

Overcome by overwhelming emotion, plenty of us reach for phone to express it – only to lose friends, jobs, and the respect of existing and potential lovers by misjudging the situation. How to make sure it doesn't happen to you? Never ever send an angry, exceedingly soppy, needy or emotional text after two drinks and don't text anyone after three drinks (bar your mother, best friend or long, long, long-term partner – and even then only to make arrangements or to be exceedingly nice) . A few other things:

● **Don't assume someone's not interested because they don't answer a text or email** Mobiles get lost, stolen, and broken. Technology isn't infallible and not everyone carries their phone wherever they go or checks their emails every hour. So if they don't answer immediately, don't assume you've upset them or they don't feel the same way.

● **Be careful with humour and innuendo** Delivered at the right time, in the right tone and with a sardonic raise of an eyebrow, that wicked one-liner about the nun and the condom might well have them holding their sides with laughter. Sadly, some – actually scratch that, most – humour doesn't translate to text and only a fraction survives email. Avoid saying anything which could be taken the wrong way. In person, it's easy to tell if you've just accidentally offended someone – and to fix it before things get into a horrible mess. A misconstrued text or email can set off a horrid chain reaction. Save important topics for when you're together.

"Call rather than text if you start to argue – talking fixes it faster"

Warning: text messaging can be addictive

Lots of people – men particularly – find it easier to express emotion via text and email because it's not face to face (hence a lot less embarrassing). Men also like it because they're often not as "in touch" with their feelings as women, so spur-of-the-moment face-to-face relationship chats render them speechless. With the written word, they get time to think about what they really want to say and how to say it. All great practice but easy to hide behind. Use text to enhance your real life relationship, not as a substitute.

hi-tech flirting

How you sit on a date says a lot. If you're having fun, make sure you look like you are!

● **Face propped up, elbow resting on table**

This is a classic boredom pose. Anyone who sits like this is at the point where they simply don't care that you know it! If this is you, be aware your date is expecting you to yawn next. If it's them, rethink just how funny the story about Aunt Marge's cupcakes really is. Leap into damage control: lean forward, touch them on the forearm, say their name, and move onto everyone's favourite topic – themselves.

● **One arm crossed, hand covering mouth**

Crossing one arm in front of you is a partial arm block – it effectively shuts people out. And we put our hands in front of our mouth to subliminally stop words we shouldn't say coming out. We also do it when we whisper something that we don't want others to lip-read. People associate it with being rude and secretive. Not a good look at any time, least of all on a date.

hand positions

● **Hands loosely clasped, on table**
This is the way I get people on a date to sit if they're nervous. It's not ideal because your arms are still crossed, but it's way better than the alternative – folding your arms or clasping your fingers together (both signs you're touchy or terrified). By sitting this way, you're getting comfort without looking tense by holding your own hand. Score big points for putting your hands on the table: this shows you have nothing to hide. Even if they're shaking like a leaf, you're much better off having them in view than sitting on them or shoving them between your thighs.

● **Hands to chest** This gesture works a treat when you're the one doing the talking – especially if you're telling a funny story which involves feigned innocence. Holding your hands up to your chest will make you look animated and honest. We put our hands to our chest to pledge allegiance and loyalty. If a guy sits like this, he wants you to know he's genuine about what he's saying. If a girl does it and is smiling broadly, like here, it's also a signal she's being open. If her hands fly quickly to her chest, however, it could mean she's being protective and you've shocked or surprised her.

hand positions

He's blocking her in
Putting one hand against the wall behind her means she's trapped under his armpit.

He's talking at her His face is too close, turning an innocent conversation into an attack.

Her drink forms a barrier With one arm crossed, she's looking away and raising her eyes to the heavens. All are signs that she's thinking "Help!".

Hand on hip
This adds to the aggressive nature of this pose. He's leaning into her intimate zone (within 15cm) and harassing rather than seducing.

Body blocks: creating private space

"Blocking" means using your body to establish a boundary around you and the person you fancy: lean your head close to theirs and you have your own vacuum in a crowded room. Not so successful: crowding instead of creating intimacy.

I'm all for fresh starts and second chances, but better be aware what you're letting yourself in for

If you see clusters of the following body language, chances are that the person's sporting a few emotional bruises, which could spell trouble. Too much eye contact: aggressive and expecting trouble. Refusing to meet your eyes: hiding something or cripplingly shy. "Blank" eyes: they've emotionally shut down. Suppressing or hiding smiles: haunted by a tragedy. Rubbing their hand on their forehead when they speak: the troubles of the world are on their shoulders. Laughing at the end of a sentence: insecure, discrediting what they've just said. Rocking or swaying: they want to run away. Smiling, nodding too much: too eager to please. Over-mirroring body language: desperate to be liked. Over-exaggerated gestures: pumped full of self-importance.

Who really sounds trustworthy?

Forget what's being said and listen to how it's delivered. If someone considers you their equal, the volume of their voice will be neither high nor low. Too loud and they're dominating, too low shrieks submissive. A harsh, ragged voice grates and repels, a too-smooth talker will make you feel suspicious (Am I being conned?). Ditto fast-talkers. The saying "fast talker" – meaning untrustworthy – is steeped in truth. We do talk faster when trying to dig ourselves out of a hole.

"Too much self-touching and stroking? They're usually self-obsessed"

Halfway through the date, escape to the loo. Take some time out to objectively review what's happening with both of you

Believe me, it'll pay off enormously. You've had time to get to know each other a little but you're not so drunk, your judgement's impaired! Ask yourself the following:

What are they saying? Ideally, the conversation will flow freely and meander in all sorts of directions as you gently probe and get to know each other. Sticking with small talk won't get you anywhere but neither will instantly diving in: if you're trading intimate secrets before the main course it's going way too fast. Aim for the odd shared intimacy and don't reveal another until they've done the same. First-date secrets should be served like ping-pong balls – traded one for one.

What's their body language telling me? Remember the Rule of Four? Look for at least four signs saying the same thing then add a huge dollop of common sense. Consider where you are – we behave differently in different circumstances. If the restaurant is formal, the date probably will be.

mid-date checklist

How important is having a laugh?

"Good sense of humour" is up there in the top three things on the partner wishlist for both sexes. What's crucial, however, isn't how much you laugh together but who makes who giggle. Recent studies based on first meetings suggest the more a man makes the woman laugh, the more interested she is in meeting him again. It was the other way around for the men: they liked the women they'd made laugh, much more than the women who'd made them laugh. How much she made him laugh didn't factor for either sex!

"If you want someone to open up to you, open up to them a little"

If it's relaxed and laid back but they're behaving like they're having tea with the Queen, they're still self-conscious and need relaxing. Don't jump to conclusions. The guy who didn't smile back when you smiled on the way back from the restroom, isn't arrogant, he's just blind without his glasses and too vain to wear them with you. Most importantly, watch for changes in body language. On a great date, the person should be moving closer, making more eye contact, and sneakily checking you out. Even simply uncrossing their arms and/or feet and looking at you more is a step in the right direction.

What signals am I sending them? Check your own body language – is it clear, positive, and an appropriate response to theirs? If you're unsure if they like you as a friend or lover, introduce touch. Lean over to touch their hand, forearm, or shoulder. If they like you and aren't shy, they'll touch you back within ten minutes or so. Later, touch them lightly on their lower back (to shift them out the way, guide them). Do they jump away from your touch or arch their back and move into it, looking over their shoulder to smile at you?

Do I want to move things on? Think objectively about what you now know about this person given the benefit of time. Are they fitting into your previous perception of them or turning out to be even better than you'd thought? Fantastic! Let it move forward. If you're getting mixed signals, consider going on somewhere else. The quickest way to change someone's attitude is to change their position by getting them to move. See if this offers a better glimpse into their personality. It could be the environment was making them feel uncomfortable or they just felt "stuck".

"It's recommended that **you touch three times**, for three seconds each time, on a **first date**"

mid-date checklist

Glasses and sunglasses

When and how people wear and remove their glasses offers a plethora of clues. Taking them off, cleaning them slowly, then putting them back on is stalling for time. A person breathing on the lenses and polishing them wants a clear view of the world. Keep removing and replacing your glasses and you may be seen as indecisive. Take them off while revealing personal information, and you let someone in. Sucking on the ends of glasses means you're either seeking comfort – or sex!

What's the best colour to wear?

The colour you wear on a date speaks its own language to the person you're with.
Black – I'm fashionable, stylish, and creative.
Red – I'm happy to be the centre of attention and unafraid of my emotions.
Pink – Hot Pink: I want to stand out from the crowd. Baby pink: Treat me gently.
Blue – Dark blue: I mean business. Light or mid-blue: I'm calm and focused.
Beige – I'm a little unsure of myself.
White – Notice me, not my clothes. All-white on men: I'm over 50 and a nerd.

For an accurate assessment of what your date's really feeling, look beyond what's being said to check out the following:

- **What's happening with their drink?**
  Good: Her fingers are stroking up and down the stem or outside of the glass. His finger is rubbing the rim. (Both are imitating how you'd like to touch each other's bits.) If she's sucking or nibbling her straw while making direct eye contact, make a move.
  Bad: If they're holding their drink chest height or higher, it's a barrier. If they don't drop it in a few minutes, give up. If they drop it but then wrap both hands around it, still give up.

- **What are they doing with their hair?**
  Good: If she removes her hair from behind her ears and shakes it loose, she's relaxing and in play mode. If he touches, musses, or smooths his hair, he's preening to look good for you.
  Bad: If she pushes her hair behind her ears, she means business. Repeatedly smoothing his hair means he's nervous.

- **How much space is there between you and your date?**
  Good: Hardly any.
  Bad: Loads.

- **What fills the space?**
  Good: Nothing. They've moved objects to clear the way.
  Bad: They've erected a wall using objects. The girl who places her handbag, drink, and jacket between you might as well be standing there in an asbestos suit.

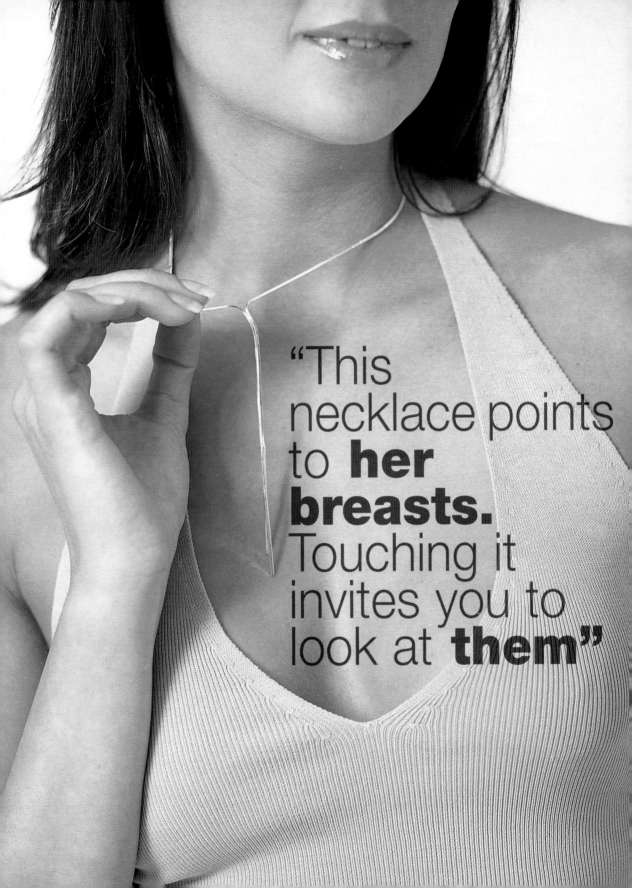

We use our eyes to assess and express – to work out how a lover is feeling and to express how we are.

The role eyes play in couple connection is extraordinary. They're nicknamed "the gateway to love" for good reason: eye contact directly influences whether we'll fall in love with someone or not. The more we like someone, the longer we lock eyes with them and the more likely the brain is to produce PEA (phenylethylamine) – a substance released when we fall in love. The more PEA floating around your system, the more likely you are to fall in love with someone. Locking eyes into a mutual lover's gaze – where we unconsciously read pupil dilations ("deep black pools" mean all is well, tiny pinprick pupils make us feel uneasy) – isn't the only thing you can do to make your date fall for you. Try any (or all) of the following:

Wide eyes Pulling back our eyelids makes our eyes look bigger, giving an affect of innocent attentiveness. Animal and human babies have big eyes in proportion to their face and few people

making eyes

Why candlelit dinners work

Our pupils dilate when we look at something we like or love – consequently, we're instinctively attracted to large pupils. Italian women in the 18th century put tiny drops of belladonna (an extract from the deadly nightshade plant) into their eyes to artificially dilate their pupils. Luckily, less drastic measures work equally as well. A good old-fashioned candlelit dinner doesn't just soften our faces, showing off our looks to best effect, it shows off our pupil dilation as well. The less light, the bigger the pupil.

"The greater the pupil **dilation,** the greater the **love"**

can resist feeling protective or nurturing of them. As adults we still feel protective when we see someone with large eyes. Widening the eyes into "look after me" works for both sexes.

Smiling eyes Think about something which makes you happy and your eyes will sparkle and dance. Instead of always smiling at a potential lover by moving your mouth into a broad smile, smile with your eyes instead. It's easier than you think (practise in front of a mirror) and research shows the more you use your eyes to send messages, the more responsive people will be to you.

Wandering eyes Being "eyeballed" – given the once-over – by some sleaze in a bar is an enormous turn-off. Feeling a much-fancied date's eyes travel lustily over your body on a deliberate but tasteful visual journey, is quite another thing. Once it's clear the two of you want more than just companionship (and are definitely heading for a snog or two), it's appropriate to let your eyes wander.

Point to your eyes Eyes follow moving things, so use your fingers (or a pen) to lift their eyes to yours. Once they're there, hold them with a five-second burst of intense gazing.

Lustful eyes Think Marilyn Monroe – lowered eyelids and raised eyebrows, mouth half-open. She effectively reproduced the expression that appears on people's faces just before they orgasm. Doing it hints at what's in store (and more on that later!)…

"The trick to flirting is to make the eyes look larger without staring"

Can you scientifically measure love?

Psychologist Zick Rubin found couples in love look at each other 75 per cent of the time when talking. In normal conversation, we look at someone for between 30 and 60 per cent. Use it to up the chances of your date falling in love with you by looking at them for 75 per cent of the time. Their brain realizes the last time someone looked at them that long in one stretch it meant they were in love, so it assumes they're in love with you as well.

making eyes

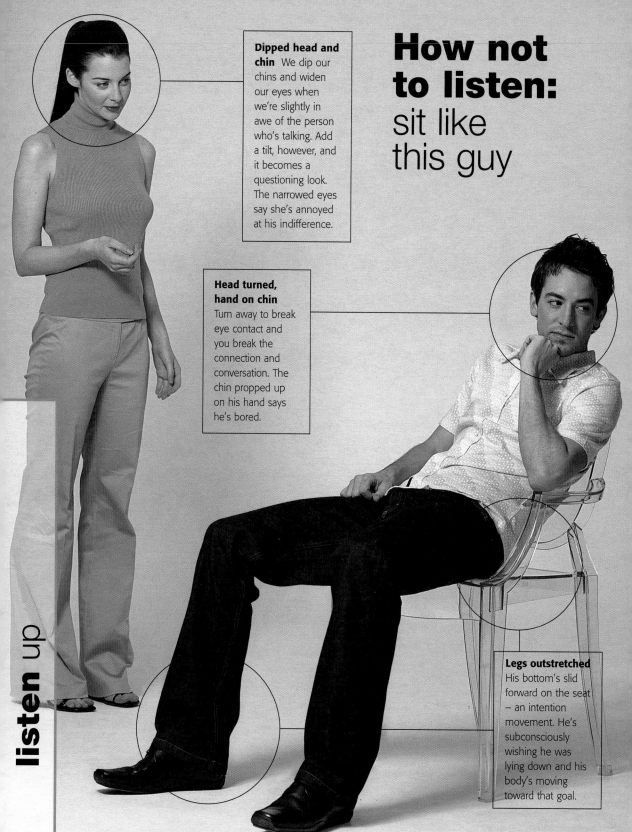

Dipped head and chin We dip our chins and widen our eyes when we're slightly in awe of the person who's talking. Add a tilt, however, and it becomes a questioning look. The narrowed eyes say she's annoyed at his indifference.

How not to listen: sit like this guy

Head turned, hand on chin Turn away to break eye contact and you break the connection and conversation. The chin propped up on his hand says he's bored.

Legs outstretched His bottom's slid forward on the seat – an intention movement. He's subconsciously wishing he was lying down and his body's moving toward that goal.

listen up

So much better!
The mirrored expressions and his mouth close to her ear are sexy and intimate

Listening is as much a skill as talking. As the saying goes, you've got two ears and one mouth – use them in proportion! It's sometimes more important to know when not to say something than it is to say the right thing. Women and men listen in different ways. Women do what's called "active listening" – throw in lots of nods and smiles and "uhuhs"; men stay still and think if they say anything at all, it'll be seen as interrupting. Because of this, each sex often misinterprets the other, assuming lack of interest when there's actually plenty.

listen up

Mismatched facial expressions How you mirror reflects how compatible you might be. If they'd "clicked", it's likely they'd look at each other, or in the same direction.

Hand on her chin The more you're on the same wavelength, the more you synchronize your actions. There's no "rhythm" between their body parts to suggest they think the same.

We like people who are like us

So if we like someone, we start "mirroring" – doing whatever it is they're doing to show we're the same. It's not conscious, but it is remarkably bonding.

Postural conflict Are their feet deliberately mismatched? If someone does the opposite to you, refusing to mirror, they are trying to be seen as different or superior: "I don't fancy you".

carbon copies

It means more if he mirrors you Generally, men are less likely than women to mirror or "echo" because they're less concerned with people liking them.

Emotional matching Their facial expressions now match. If they go on to mirror each other – doing the same things at the same time – it's a sign they're on the same emotional wavelength.

Postural matching It's no wonder they're now holding hands. Mirroring works two ways: the stronger the "click", the more you do it; and the more you do it, the stronger the connection becomes.

carbon copies

People **are** fiercely territorial

We mentally divide the space and objects around us into "our" side and "their" side, guarding what's "ours" ferociously. Except, of course, when the person who's invading our space is someone we want to come (much) closer. Then the whole thing becomes an elaborate – and enjoyable – game.

"To see who's interested move the **salt shaker"**

space invaders

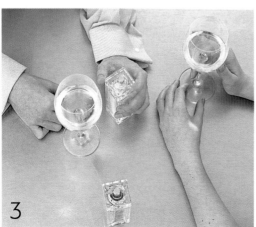

1

Start playing with an object on the table
Make sure it's on "your" side or central –
a wine glass, a toothpick holder, or salt
or pepper shaker. Lean forward slightly
in your chair and absent-mindedly fondle
it with both hands.

2

Surreptitiously push it over their side
Slide it just over the invisible line that divides
the two of you. Now take your hands away,
lean back slightly, and continue chatting.
How they respond to this simple move
is very interesting.

3

Watch how they react
If they're not keen, they'll instinctively push
it back over the line to your side – feeling
uncomfortable and sensing you're trying to
get close without really knowing why. If,
instead, they leave it there (good) or (there
is a God) hold it, it's likely they want to
rev things up.

4

Lean forward with forearms on the table
Wrap your fingers around your wine glass
and start pushing that over the line to their
side. The person who fancies you will also
lean forward, and push their glass, or another
object, to your side of the table. If they lean
back and keep their hands in their lap, order
dessert. Comfort food is in order!

Hold hands
to find out how someone feels about you

Linked fingers (*top*) mean they want to mesh every body part. It's much more significant than the simple palm-to-palm clasp (*bottom*), the trademark of a settled couple, showing affection and acceptance. Why? It's much harder to break the hold and usually means you've got a firm grip on each other and are reluctant to let go. Got your eye on someone who's attached and spot them holding hands like this? Give up now. It's the sign of a couple who don't tend to let anything come between them.

Not so the person who keeps their fingers straight so you're forced to hang onto the tips (*middle*). This is the hand-hold of a commitment-phobe. You're clinging on but they're poised to break contact at any moment, keeping a physical distance which nearly always translates to an emotional chasm.

How someone holds hands also reveals who's the boss. The person whose thumb lands on top, is usually in the power position (in the top image, it's the girl). The direction of the palm is also telling. If they turn your hand so their palm faces back (like the man in the main picture, *opposite*), they're in the front, control position. A kinder interpretation is they're being protective, but be warned! Test which is which by twisting your hand so that yours is "in front". If they quickly turn it back again, they're intent on being boss.

hand-holding clues

"The palm direction **says this** man is the boss of the **relationship"**

They want to kiss you if...

They lick their lips Both sexes lick their lips when faced with something arousing.
They keep touching their mouth When turned on, our lips are engorged. This makes us conscious of them so we touch them.
They eat or drink suggestively Eating an ice-cream, then licking fingers afterwards – they're trying to advertise their talents.
They put their head close to yours Nearly always an invitation to kiss.
They look at you with head tilted They're already getting into position!

Was the kiss welcome?

Start by brushing soft, relaxed lips lightly against theirs, mouth slightly open. You'll know immediately if they're interested. It's not good news if their lips clench shut, they involuntarily pull back, or their lips, and mouth feel cool. Keep going if everything feels hot, they part their lips and lean toward the kiss. If one hand comes up to cradle the back of your head, they're particularly keen. The more passionate they want the kiss to be, the further they'll part their lips. People kiss the way they'd like to be kissed. Kiss passively let them take the lead, then simply imitate whatever they do.

According to legend, the French kiss was invented by medieval knights to find out if their wives had been secretly supping at the mead barrel while they were gone. Rather amusing when you consider few of us would pass the alcohol detection test now! Most people need some Dutch courage to pucker up for the first time with someone special because they realize how tremendously significant that first kiss is.

Mouths are almost as complex as eyes, and kissing is where all the sexual synergy starts. Kiss someone and you can tell how they feel about you romantically and sexually, how they're likely to be in bed, how they'll perform oral sex – and whether you're a good biological match. Trust your first kiss: it's like swapping a biological business card. Sebaceous glands in the mouth and corners of your lips release semiochemicals, designed to stimulate sexual excitement. These combine with your own unique saliva fingerprint and the end result is passed on during kissing. If canny old Mother Nature doesn't determine it to be a good genetic mix, the first kiss won't taste or smell right for either of you, stopping the chances of things moving forward. Few people will pursue someone if the first kiss doesn't spark sexual fireworks. It's perhaps for this reason that the drive to kiss appears to be innate – something we do instinctively. Over 90 per cent of all peoples on record kiss, with the world's most frequent kissers being Westerners and Hindus.

"If they start to chew, drink, or smoke faster, **they want to kiss you**"

Tracey's Top Tips

Don't turn up late

Time is a powerful non-verbal communicator – the more important you are, the less you have of it. People of higher status keep people waiting, people of lower status don't dare to. It doesn't matter if the train was late, you couldn't find your keys, or a neighbour cornered you near the letterbox, the message you send if you're late on a date is: "This isn't important to me. I don't care as much as you do."

Psychologically strip

It's a what-you-see-isn't-necessarily-what-you-get technique. Once you've established a certain image on the date, you then peel back a layer to reveal a totally unexpected side to yourself. Ms. Innocence who turns out to be quite feisty. The career girl who turns out to be shy. We all like to think we know the "real" person, and hidden depth is attractive.

Look for the lover's steeple

If, in the early stages, someone plants their elbow, then leans forward with splayed fingers, inviting you to touch their fingertips, they're symbolically merging you together to see if you "fit". Have you both met your matching half?

Look beneath the mask

Don't take everything at face value. If someone seems stiff and oddly false, keep them talking and watch for "microexpressions" – fleeting glimpses that give away how they're really feeling. Shy and unsure people do what's called "masking" – a false expression deliberately composed to disguise a (usually inappropriate) expression (fear, insecurity) behind it. Watch celebrities' faces when the Oscar goes to someone else. They arrange their features into a smile but you can see the expression of disappointment lurking underneath.

Get them to lie down

A picnic in the park with both of you lying on a rug isn't just romantic and sexy, it's the best way to get someone to open up. There's a reason why shrinks have couches – people behave differently lying down to sitting up. We remember more and are more reflective because we're less inclined to move, leaving us more likely to concentrate. We're more responsive to new suggestions and to closely examining a topic – like your future as a couple, maybe?

the**couple**

"Their body will often tell you they're unhappy before they tell you themselves"

So you've been a good student and flirted your way into the heart of someone special. Great! Now all you have to do is keep their attention and devotion for as long as you'd like to stay together. There are three things you need to do to keep a relationship healthy:

Listen Not just to what's being said but to the subtext of what's really being said. "I'm sick of staying in with a takeaway" really means "We're in a rut. We need to do something exciting".

Watch Watch how they stand with you. Compare it to how they stand with their best friend, people you know they don't like very much. Pay attention to how they sit, walk, move when they're in different moods. How they use their hands, touch their hair, smile, laugh, and frown. Don't just teach yourself the basics of body language, become an expert in their individual gestures and mannerisms so you can interpret their moods and feelings without them even saying a word.

Touch You cannot be close emotionally, without being close physically. Stop touching and you'll stop loving.

Does your lover look like you?

A big tick if the answer is yes. Go out with someone who looks like you and they're four times more likely to fall in love with you! Researchers measured a selection of in-love couples and found they were four times more likely to share the same length earlobes, lung volumes, wrist and ankle measurements, distances between their eyes, and length of middle fingers. We appear to be attracted to people who look like us because we feel comfortable with things we're frequently exposed to – even faces.

reading relationships

So you've met, kissed, and are officially a couple. Now what? How do you make sure things run smoothly?

The worst thing you can do is adopt a head-in-the-sand approach to your relationship, kidding yourself things are going brilliantly when they're clearly not, by refusing to acknowledge signs of trouble. I'd strongly suggest you do the opposite: stand back and take an objective look at what's going on at regular intervals. Don't assume your partner is happy, ask them. What would they like more or less of? Check their body language to check their words and actions match. It takes courage to admit all isn't well or you're in a rut. Sometimes their body will tell you before they do.

reading relationships

The twelve stages of sex.
We think we're individuals, yet most Western couples climb the same sexual staircase to the bedroom.

We might skip a stage or two or get them slightly out of order, but the majority of couples are remarkably predictable, following the same path from meeting to full sex as the rest of the world. Why do we follow the order so faithfully? We're influenced by what society perceives as taboo: the places we touch first are the least risky, those we touch last – the genitals – are the most frowned upon. Zoologist Desmond Morris is the man who charted the path from pair formation to copulation. What isn't predictable is how long it takes you to go from start to finish. Years, months, weeks, or mere minutes – that's the part which is totally in your control!

1. Eye to body We spot each other from a distance and the eyes feed the brain sexual information. Each of you rate each other on a scale of "yes please" to "not if they were the last person alive".

the **path** to pleasure

"The first touch is often the most erotic"

Century-old sexploits

If you think we're uptight and prudish about sex today, spare a thought for gynaecologists of the past. Three hundred years ago, they were required to crawl into their pregnant patient's bedroom on their hands and knees to perform a vaginal examination, so that she wouldn't see the owner of the fingers that were to touch her in such a forbidden place. Things eventually "progressed" to the point where they were able to stand, but with lights off, forced to deliver a baby by groping beneath the bedclothes.

Assuming you both make the grade, you're off and running.

2. Eye to eye You look at them, they look at you, but you check each other out in turn rather than simultaneously. If you're still happy with what you see, eventually the glances cross over, become lingering, and one of you adds a smile.

3. Voice to voice You meet and talk – risky business! Everything from your accent, voice tone, and speed of speech influence how you'll come across. Your personalities start to take form and a close-up view means both or either of you think twice about taking it further.

4. Hand to hand The first touch is often a handshake, an accidental touch, or one of you grabbing the other's hand to cross the street. The contact moves from brief to prolonged, then neither of you let go. Simply holding hands has never felt (nor will ever feel, if you stay together) quite so exciting and sensual.

5. Arm to shoulder This is the first time your bodies come into direct contact. Usually, it's his arm which goes around her shoulders (height differences as well as society's view on who makes the first move). The reason why the shoulder embrace comes first is because it's common among friends, so it's the least threatening hug of all. Halfway between close friendship and love, there's still a get-out clause. You can leave with dignity intact if the signals have been misread.

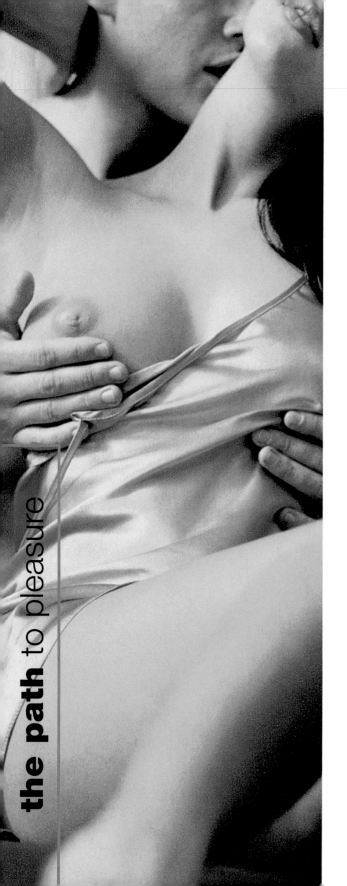

6. Arm to waist Moving from the "friendly" shoulder to the "amorous" waist, the mood changes significantly. You're working your way down the body to be closer to the genitals.

7. Mouth to mouth Kissing comes next, combined with an oh-so-delicious full-frontal hug! This is the bravest step so far – there's no pretending you both now just want friendship. We also see the first signs of sexual arousal. If you've been doing some serious flirting and drawn out seduction, kissing alone can be a tremendous turn-on.

8. Hand to head It doesn't sound particularly sexy or significant, but wait, there's more! It's the first step to caressing the body plus it's a sign of intimacy. In the majority of cases, hands stroking hair remind you both you're not just there purely for sex. Nevertheless, we tend to move rather rapidly past this point to the next, more exciting bit…

9. Hand to body Usually, it's his hand on her breast. It starts out as a tentative "May I?" stroke and progresses to a more sexually aggressive, firmer kneading motion. Heavy breathing, vaginal secretions, and erections are also usually happening at this point.

10. Mouth to breast The mood shifts to intensely passionate because once you've decided to go this far, it could mean you'll take it through to the conclusion of penetrative sex and orgasm.

"Some men can move from zero arousal to orgasm in a mere three minutes"

11. Hand to genitals It starts with his hand outside her knickers, moving to inside and (finally!) the longed-for flesh-on-flesh contact of naughty bits. This is often the point where she will also touch his penis: through his trousers or by slipping a hand inside to touch directly. Both of you then settle into a rhythmic rubbing which simulates the thrusting of intercourse. Orgasm may or may not occur.

12. Genitals to genitals Once you start having regular sex together, you'll add another stage between this and intercourse: mouth to genitals (oral sex). But for first-time sex, most of us move straight to penetration – and rather swiftly onto orgasm.

"The average woman takes 20 minutes to orgasm from a cold start"

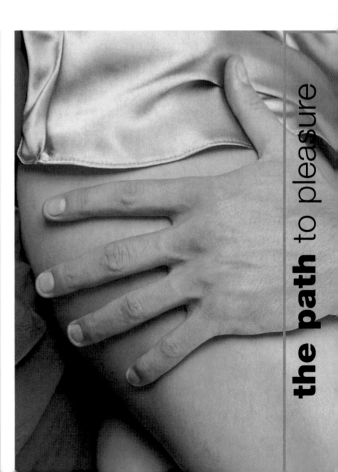

the **path** to pleasure

Our arm
position reveals who wears the trousers

Powerful people tend to hug higher on the body, wrapping arms around the shoulders; the more submissive aim lower, often opting for the waist. If it's her hugging him in this manner – like in the picture opposite – it's a take-control sexual statement, which says "Come here, I want to ravish you". The fact he's accepting her neck-hold also speaks volumes. Each sex has "no-go" zones, particularly when touching in public. Some are obvious (like breasts), others are the result of being touched differently as children.

Men often don't like being touched on the hair, face, and neck because as young boys, they hated being "fussed over" by Mum, who would constantly fix ruffled hair and skewed collars, setting the seed for feeling uncomfortable when touched on the upper body later in life. Him accepting a strong neck-hold means she's well and truly accepted. If it's done in public, add adored. Sadly, full body-hugs are like kisses – the longer you're in a relationship, the less frequent they become. Eventually they fade to purely "break-and-remake": a way to say hello and goodbye.

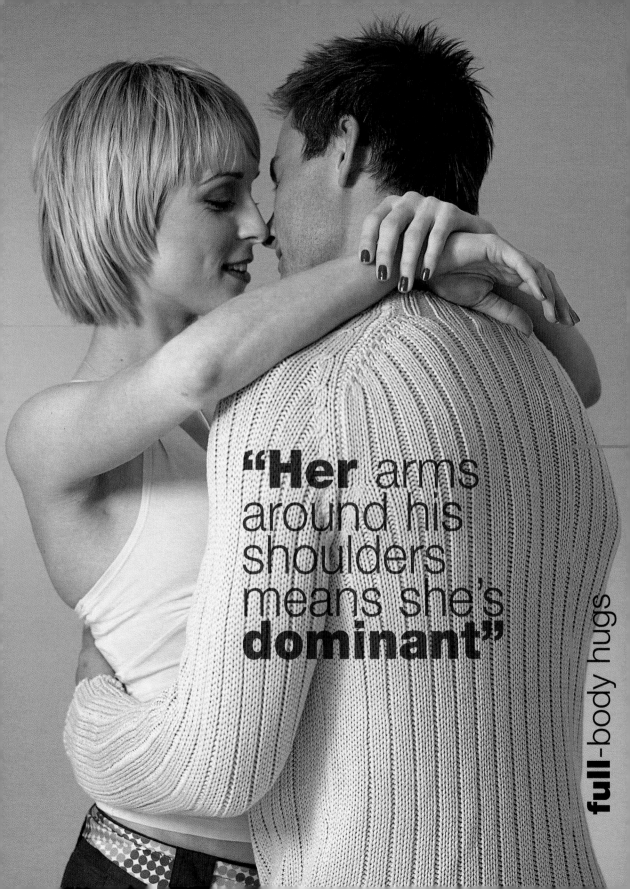

"**Her** arms around his shoulders means she's **dominant**"

full-body hugs

Smile and your partner smiles with you! A smile can often fix a problem before it becomes one

Fact: the more you smile, the more people like you. This applies to your relationship as well. Flash a happy/sexy/cheeky/naughty/seductive/suggestive/supportive smile frequently at your partner and it should be obvious you've got more chance of keeping them happy than if you serve up the equivalent in scowls. Caught up in the stresses and pressures of life, however, it's all too easy to forget the value of smiling.

The truth is, though, that we were born to smile. Even blind and deaf children grin, smile, and laugh, without ever having seen or heard others do it. Smiling is contagious. Smile at someone you're annoyed with and tension instantly dissolves the second they smile back. Refuse to smile if they offer you a tentative one, and the relationship may never recover. As Desmond Morris says, the simple failure to return a smile, between two great rulers, can lead to war and destruction.

happy ever after

The two most effective attention seekers

As babies, crying and smiling have a basic function: crying says "I need attention", smiling up at your Mum guarantees she'll want to give it to you. As we grow older, the attention we're seeking might shift focus, but the means of getting it remain the same. A cry still gets us a cuddle and a smile gets us noticed, loved, and (most importantly of all) laid!

"Anything that involves the mouth transmits pseudo-genital signals"

This is one situation where faking it is a very good idea. Experiments show if people are asked to smile and are then shown pictures of various events, they tend to report that the pictures made them happy. Others, shown the same pictures, but asked to frown before seeing them, report experiencing feelings of annoyance and even anger. Not only are you better off offering up a weak, strained smile than none at all, but faking a smile can result in a real one because the position of our facial muscles feeds information back to our brain. Stretch your mouth into a smile and the brain registers you're smiling and releases the hormonal response that usually accompanies it – chemicals that make you feel happy. Before you know it, that insincere grimace has transformed into a genuine beam! Which is a good thing because although fake smiles really are better than nothing, most people can instinctively spot one without really knowing why.

The differences are subtle but significant. A fake smile stays fixed in position while a real one flashes on and off. Fake smiles look round rather than oblong and appear lop-sided rather than even. The lips look tight and stretched rather than fleshy and relaxed, teeth are bared rather than exposed naturally. Most telling: fake smiles don't "reach" the eyes. When we smile broadly our eyes crinkle and change shape, our nose looks wider and spreads broadly across the face, and our cheeks ball and lift.

"The quickest way to up your sex appeal is to laugh and smile more"

The link between laughter and sex

A belly-laugh relaxes the body and reduces tension. Laughter releases natural drugs into the bloodstream, which make us feel pleasure. We feel more confident, optimistic, and attractive after a good laugh with good reason: our bodies are in a similar state of arousal to sexual arousal. We're breathless, our heart rate increases, circulation is heightened, and the skin has a faint flush. Perhaps this is why laughing with someone for a few minutes can bond us more effectively than talking with them for hours.

happy ever after

Public poses

How someone stands next to you in public is very significant. As a general rule, the more infatuated they are, the more "mate guard" and "mate retention" signs they'll show. Both are simply public displays of affection – like holding hands - which "guard" (warn others you're already spoken for) and "retain" (keep you feeling loved and cared for).

touching in public

Lots of space
The farther apart you stand in public, the more distant you're likely to be in private. Look at their trunk posture: a good indicator of feelings. They're both stiff and reluctant to "melt" together.

His foot is running away
Her feet walk toward him – she's happy to be with him and would like to get closer. His foot points away – he's planning to escape the first chance he gets.

Touching foreheads
It's impossible to interact with anyone else while standing like this, so it's a rather effective excluding action that separates the couple from the rest of the world. For that reason, it's favoured by young couples rather than the older and more socially conscious.

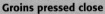

Groins pressed close
The closer the groin, the more sexually satisfied the couple; touching chests means they're also emotionally happy. Lots of space between upper bodies is a sign your hearts aren't connecting.

Her knee between his legs This can mean sexual longing or a longing to knee someone where it hurts! If all else is well, relax. If you're talking emotively, take it as a threat of what would happen if you put a foot wrong.

touching in public

1

2

3

Hands can
be just as expressive as words

We use "baton gestures" to mark the points we want to emphasize when talking – and backing up the spoken message with body language is never a bad idea! People prefer communicating with someone whose hands are lively than someone who keeps their hands still, simply because they're easier to understand. If you're having trouble getting your point across, add some baton gestures while talking and see an instant difference!

1. "Let's all calm down here!" The palm down gesture is used by the level headed. It reflects their urge to lower the intensity of emotion being expressed.

2. "Not for me, thanks!" Turn your palms frontward and it turns into a protest. The hands are held up to protect the speaker and/or to push away something distasteful that is coming their way (a thought, suggestion, or person). The general message is clear: "I'm rejecting whatever it is you're offering me."

3. "And another thing!" Mum shook her finger at us to tell us off as kids, so no one's too thrilled when someone does it to us as an adult. With our finger poised as a symbolic stick ready to hit, a raised forefinger is seen as hostile.

"Talk with your hands to double your chance of being heard"

4

4. "Absolutely not!" "I won't have it." The hand scissor is fairly self-explanatory: do it and you're cutting off whatever is being forced on you.

5. "Give me what I need to understand this" With palms pulling back toward the chest, it's as though you're hugging an invisible person. You're attempting to embrace an idea or pull the person talking closer to you. It means you need more positives to convince you to move over to their side.

6. "Let's cut to the chase" Using your hands to chop through the air like an axe means you want the person to cut through the confusion of the situation and do whatever it is that you're suggesting.

5

6

walking in step

Take a stroll
to discover if you're well-matched

Walking around the block with someone is a quick and remarkably accurate way to find out if you're long-term compatible. If you're striding ahead and they're ambling along, stopping to smell the flowers, give up now. Fast-paced and slow-paced people have to battle a multitude of problems to make things work. The couple who walk in step – forming mirror images of each other by adopting the same pace with the same leg leading – have a rosy future. It shows you're both travelling at the same speed through life.

Once you're firmly established as a couple, "postural matching" remains an effective way to check you're on course. Walking in step is a sign of shared common goals; sharing the same walking style hints at similar personalities. One of the first symptoms of a couple in crisis is their tendency to suddenly stand, sit, or walk differently. This is our subconscious trying to separate us from a merged "we", back into individuals. We're emotionally preparing for a possible break-up. The less physical mirroring you do, the less bonded you feel and the better able you are to cope if you lose your other half.

Turning toward each other

Completely turning your head to face a partner while walking is significant. Our natural inclination is to look ahead to make sure we don't bump into anything! This says, "I'm more concerned with where we're going together".

A guiding hand

His hand in the small of her back means he wants to keep track on where she's going. It's a positive sign. Not so the person who holds your hand behind their back. It can mean they're subconsciously trying to hide your relationship.

Swinging arms

Shows a nice, relaxed walking style. Simply moving your hand away from your body can mean the difference between looking open and looking closed (compare his right arm *opposite*).

Neither one leads

Which means an equal relationship. If your partner always walks ahead of you, they're the ones guiding your love in whatever direction they choose.

walking in step

Stand like
this if you
want to show
they're yours

Placing one **hand on your partner's lower stomach** *(top, left)* is either a proprietorial, protective gesture (warning other people off) or a sexual invitation of things to come (literally). Slipping a hand down from the chest to just above the pubic bone puts it in a favourite resting place for the hands of new lovers.

An open, flat **palm planted on his chest** *(middle, left)* pressed against the heart suggests honesty of emotion. Celebrity couples often use the hand-on-heart gesture to try to convince a dubious public their love is sincere. Do it to show your partner your feelings are real.

Better pray they are if your partner moves to **hug** you **from behind** *(bottom, left)*. A thinly disguised "You're mine. Let me drag you back to my cave", it's a fiercely passionate display at best. At worst: a sign jealousy and possessive behaviour may well lurk around the corner.

Putting your **hand on someone's bottom** *(opposite)* announces to all and sundry that this is your sexual partner. It's naughtily playful since fingers are now straying into intimate zones. Confident women don't think twice before slipping a hand into their man's jean pocket, but a shy girl wouldn't dream of it.

Two-thirds of all hugs we give or receive are romantic or sexual – it's a primitive need to be touched and hugged.

But there's a lot more to a hug than simply wrapping your arms around someone…

Hug tight but not too tightly Hanging on tight usually indicates a subconscious wish to keep the person permanently close, both physically and emotionally. Easy does it, though. There's a huge difference between lightly draping one of your limbs over theirs and clutching onto them like they're the last life-raft on the *Titanic*.

Close hugging in public This is a dramatic "tie-sign" which indicates a strong personal bond. While lots of us hug hello and goodbye, only young lovers hug constantly. If you're still doing it years in, go to the front of the class.

Close hugging from behind It's often a highly sexual gesture – particularly from a man to a woman – because it puts your most intimate parts (genitals and bottoms) into intimate zones

hugs and cuddles

A pat on the back

Where people put their hands and what they do with them during hugging is remarkably informative. The more intense the feeling, the tighter and longer they'll hang on. If someone pats you on the back during a hug, it's part reassurance, part "OK, let go now". By patting someone on the back, we're secretly letting them know the hug is over.

"The only hug deemed "acceptable" man to man is a shoulder hug"

(in position, ready for intercourse). Only extremely close, tactile friends would hug closely from behind. Otherwise it's safe to assume the person wants – or is already having – sex with you. Hugging from behind can also mean the person feels submissive: you're in front, they're clinging to your coat-tails. The more upright you stand while they're hugging you, the more emotionally distant you are from them. This is a definitive pose of one who loves (behind) and one who is loved (in front). If you lean back into their arms, the pose turns back into being positive.

What hugging says about your sex life The couple who enjoy lots of full body hugs are usually having good, satisfying sex on a regular basis. If your hands often sneak under your coat or clothing to ensure even closer contact between torsos, you're in especially good shape. If sex is bad or infrequent, hugs are usually the first to go. They're embarrassing – an acute reminder your bodies should be touching for other reasons, not just affection. Staying physically close by hugging, also ensures you both continue to release oxytocin, the hormone responsible for wanting to snuggle.

What else is happening? Do they actively hug you back – or do their arms rest loosely and half-heartedly on your shoulders? Facial expressions are also important. Smiling during a close hug invariably signals true happiness simply because the person you're hugging can't see your face. The emotion's not for show, it's for real. Nestling your face into their neck implies a desire for security.

"The more connection points in a hug, the closer you are or want to be"

How does their hug rate on the hug-o-meter?

Side-on hug: they're standing beside you and giving you a squeeze. They're unsure of how the hug will be interpreted and want you to know it's non-threatening.

A half hug: their bottom half and feet are pulled away. They want to ensure no pelvic contact, which means they're uncomfortable with hugging, don't fancy you, or just don't like you.

A sexy hug: their feet are super-close, their pelvis is thrust forward rather than back. Get a room: they want your body!!

hugs and cuddles

"Men lie to make themselves look good, women lie to make other people feel good"

Don't get so caught up in the body language you forget to listen to what your partner says. These are clues they're covering something up:

Too short answers Lack of detail could mean they're trying not to drop themselves in it. Ask them to elaborate on the situation and they'll simply repeat what they've already told you.

Too long answers They're babbling or trying to confuse the lie by giving way too much information.

Denying rather than confirming "I wasn't with Angela", rather than "I was with Dave".

Verbal distancing Liars use "I", "me", or "mine" less in an attempt to emotionally distance themselves. "The match was great" rather than "I enjoyed the match".

You won't believe this, but… Well aware of how dodgy it all sounds, they figure if they acknowledge it rather than pretend it's all perfectly plausible, you might just fall for it.

Answering a question with a question They're buying time and also trying to find out what you think before they tell you what they think.

danger signs

Why guilt-free liars often get away with it

Pretty much all the lying "evidence" you'll be told to watch out for by people like me is based on a premise which may or may not be true. We assume the person feels guilty about lying, so will behave the way any anxious, tense person would when put under pressure. While this is true in the majority of cases, plenty of people feel zero remorse about what they got up to or lying about it. If this is the case, all of the so-called "clues" mean nothing. This is why it's essential not to rely purely on gut reaction but to look at all the evidence: body language, conversational clues, and past history.

Both sexes lie to cover up an affair, and we get worse, not better, at spotting deceit the more we know someone

Why? Because we become over-confident that we'll spot the signs and less objective. She doesn't know it, but the man in this picture is almost certainly lying. He's rubbing his ear (he doesn't want to hear himself lie), the hand flat on the sofa means he's grounding himself (he's literally trying to "get a grip"), he's avoiding direct eye contact, and he's not touching her (people find it almost impossible to lie while touching).

danger signs

We lie to a third of the people we meet each day. But we mostly lie to impress our lovers

● **The nose touch** If we're savvy enough to realize holding fingers or a hand over our mouth gives us away, we'll divert the gesture and end up touching our nose instead. Watch a tape of Bill Clinton on trial for his affair with Monica Lewinsky and you'll see that when he tells the truth he hardly touches his nose at all. When he lied about his affair, he touches his nose an average of once every four minutes.

● **Disguised collar-pull** An inexperienced liar will often pull their shirt collar away from the neck. Why? In most cases, lying causes stress and anxiety which makes our body temperature rise. Clothing feels tight and restrictive and we perspire. Pulling a collar away from the skin stops that trickle of sweat tickling and lets cool air circulate. A practiced liar realizes this gesture might give him away, as does a far more subtle version of the original *(below)*.

are they lying to me?

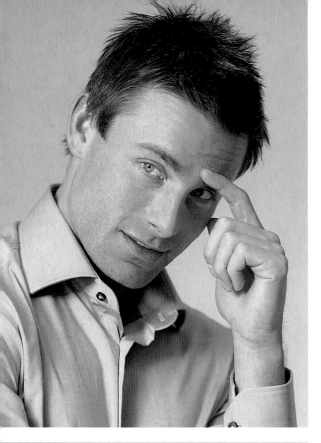

● **The eye cover** When we see something we don't wish to look at – like a lover's face, hurt and confused, searching ours for signs of deceit – we'll try to cover our vision. Putting our head in our hands and completely covering our eyes would mean the game's over, but by putting one hand up to our brow and looking down and away we've accomplished roughly the same thing. Men will often rub one eye vigorously and look to the floor when lying. Women tend to use a smaller, gentler rubbing notion (to avoid smudging eye make-up) and look to the ceiling.

● **The mouth guard** We sometimes cover our mouths when lying because even we can't believe what rubbish is coming out of it! If they're talking to you and covering their mouth, chances are they're the ones lying. If they do it while you're (fast) talking, they think you're the one talking nonsense. As a very, very general rule, the more hand-to-face gestures a person makes, the more likely it is they are lying to you. Given that we only detect 56 per cent of the lies we're told, you need to be on your guard more often than you think. All the signs are there!

are they lying to me?

Is she happy with you?

Feeling insecure and not sure if your new lover is as happy as you are? A no-fail way for a guy to find out if a girl's happy to be with him and happy sexually is to place a cupped hand on her bottom when in public. If she arches her back to press her bottom toward your touch, lifts a shoulder, and turns her head to deliver a killer smile, she's got no complaints!

Is he infatuated?

If he prefers putting an arm around your waist, rather than holding hands, it's a good sign. Hand-holding stops your bodies getting close, hugging around the waist means your sides can press against each other. Also significant: hugging you with hands completely encircling your waist, fingers intertwined. Not only does this pull you as close as possible, the knitted fingers mean he's fiercely protective and doesn't want to let you go. Consider yourself adored!

too keen, too fast

The quickest way to send a longed-for lover running for the hills is to be over-eager and fast-forward the relationship. Hanging onto their every word and body part and talking wistfully about weekends away and moving to the country because it'd be better for the kids, isn't a terribly good idea three months in, let alone on date two. But it's not just words which will giveaway just how desperately you want them to like you. Be careful you don't do any of the following:

- **Standing too close, touching too much** Invading someone's space and man-handling them *(opposite)* makes most people feel suffocated, crowded, and mauled rather than appreciated. Back off. Give them space to breathe!
- **Laughing, smiling, nodding too much** It's a good idea to avoid doing anything in excess at the start of the relationship because even "good" characteristics can take on ominous doormat overtones. Too much of all of the above will make you appear overly compliant (aka a pushover).
- **Excessive face-watching and over-mirroring** We check the faces of people we love to make sure they're happy. The odd glance shows you care; barely removing your eyes from their face is overkill. Ditto mirroring their body language. We copy other people's gestures/poses subconsciously in a bid to bond with them. Doing it deliberately in a *Single White Female* way will simply make them think you're weird!

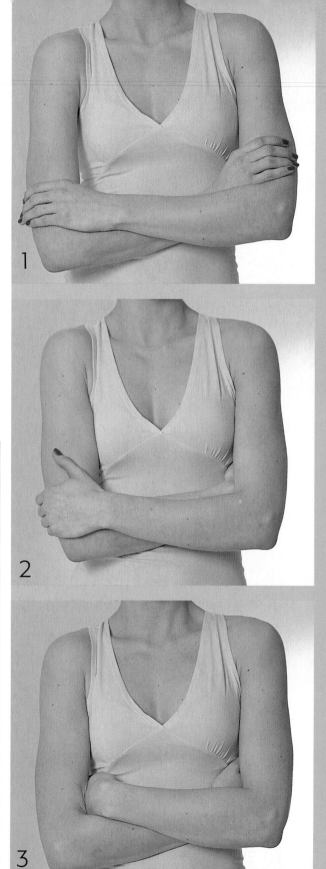

1

2

3

What's **your** partner really saying?

Sooner or later, you're going to have a row. It might be a minor disagreement or it might be the mother of all arguments. Here's a tip: don't just rely on words when it happens – look at your partner's body language to check how the discussion is going. They might well be nodding and saying "Yes, you're right". But if their hands are balled into tight fists it's not all right at all. Watch for the following:

1. The standard arm cross If you're talking to your partner and they fold their arms, they've disagreed with what you've just said. If you're about to have a heavy discussion and their arms are crossed before you talk, you've got your work cut out: they've already decided to respond negatively. Crossed arms mean a closed mind. It's essential they uncross them, so hand them something like a drink.

2. Hand gripping the arm Not only are they defensive, they're determined to hang on to their bad mood or attitude by taking a firm hold. Settle in for the long haul – it's going to be hard work.

3. The reinforced arm cross This person is angry. They're hiding their hands because they're in tight fists and people make a fist for one reason: to punch – literally or metaphorically. If your partner does this, stop talking and take a 20-minute time-out. This is how long it takes for the body to calm down.

"Having a row? What does their body tell you?"

4. Hands hidden in pockets This pose shrieks discomfort. People shove their hands deep in their pockets when they want to hide something: they're nervous, lying, or highly uncomfortable. With one small adjustment – the thumbs left out – the message changes completely. Confident people put their thumbs on display.

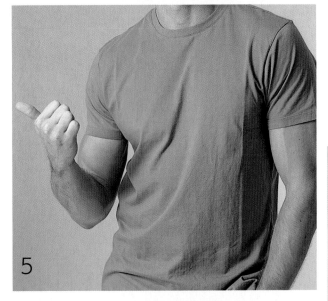

5. The disrespectful thumb If you're talking to someone and they lift a thumb, cock it towards you, and say something to a friend, you can bet it was something derogatory. If your partner uses it during an argument, they're being patronising.

6. Thumbs up One word: arrogant. The folded arms mean negativity or defensiveness, the thumbs pointing upward signal superiority. They believe they are in the right.

fighting fair

Eskimo kisses appear less intimate than a mouth-to-mouth snog, but are actually more so as eye contact is maintained

A loving rather than sexual gesture, we rub noses only with people we are extremely fond of. It hints at a carefree, playful happiness with little relationship angst. Kissing our partner's forehead is another highly affectionate gesture, but one which has a more protective feel. Watch men who have just found out they're about to be (happy) fathers. Their first response is nearly always to put their hand over their partner's stomach. The second is to plant a kiss on her forehead. Kissing on the lips seems too sexual for her new role so they revert to a parental gesture.

couple kisses

"Touching foreheads and a soul-searching gaze means trust and loyalty"

couple kisses

"In 90 minutes you can work out what makes **someone tick**"

Tracey's Top Tips

Love at first sight is possible...

If you're good at people-reading and interpreting body language, you can work out someone's core character in a few hours. It's entirely plausible to trust a notion that you "click", without even knowing that person's last name or what they do for a living.

...but not probable

What isn't possible to discover instantly is whether you could make each other happy for the rest of your lives. Even seeing it spelt out like this makes most logical people realize just how dopey the concept of love at first sight really is. Delicious, but dopey! It's easy to confuse intensity of emotion with love. Think about how many past lovers you cared passionately about and it becomes clear that you need more than strong emotion to make love last.

Falling and being in love are different

The first bit's far easier -- and to be brutally honest, loads more fun. Your body is flooded with addictive, intoxicating feel-good neurotransmitters like dopamine and serotonin. Sadly, this conquer-the-world feeling only lasts a maximum of 18 months, when all the "love drugs" dry up. They are replaced by other chemicals which make you feel like snuggling and settling, but it's around about then that lots of you have to face the truth: does this person keep me happy on a more real, day-to-day level or was it the in-love sensation that kept me interested?

Liking is as important as loving

Some people bring out the best in us, other people the worst. If you find yourself loving someone but not liking them terribly much, you've got a chemistry/chemical connection but a compatibility mismatch. Narcissistic, selfish beings we are, we actually don't fall in love with other people, we fall in love with the feelings we get when we're with them. If it doesn't feel good, and they don't make you feel good, don't go there!

Body language at a glance

While you should never judge on one gesture alone, it is useful to have a broad idea of what certain actions might mean. I'm generalizing here and making all sorts of assumptions, but here it is anyway: a quick reference guide which should come in handy. Just remember to apply The Rule of Four: look for at least four simultaneous gestures saying the same thing.

GESTURES

LEGS AND FEET

one leg tucked under they're listening and settling in.

feet flat on ground and pointing toward you they're honest, open, and interested in you.

legs crossed loosely at the knees quiet confidence.

legs stretched out in front of them could either mean they're comfortable and relaxed or they're trying to dominate by taking up as much space as possible.

both legs and arms loosely crossed warning sign, back off.

both arms and legs tightly crossed defensive and tense.

ankles crossed prim and proper or holding back negative emotion.

wrapping legs or feet around legs of chair insecure, waiting to be "tripped up" and hanging on for dear life.

sitting with one leg under the other they're a free spirit, informal.

crossing and recrossing legs if it's a female doing it, and it's in a flirting situation, she's sending a blatant sexual invitation. In other situations where a person looks anxious, it could mean they're lying.

man crossing his legs he's hostile and forming a barrier.

hugging knees to chest this person needs a hug.

tapping feet, jiggling leg they want to leave but feel they can't.

perched on edge of seat they're avidly listening to what you're saying or they're ready to leave.

feet not flat on the floor if their feet aren't flat and steady, chances are they aren't either.

sitting on someone's desk at work a blatant power play.

man sitting with his legs spread he's doing a crotch display, subliminally highlighting the "me Tarzan, you Jane" sexual differences.

swinging the top leg if it's occasional, it could be a ploy to draw attention to the legs. If it's a constant up-down motion, the person is bored.

woman swinging leg and clasping knee she's feminine, playful, and girly.

stroking or smoothing the thighs if done in a deliberate, controlled way with smooth strokes, they want you to notice them. If the person is wiping their palms repetitively on their upper thigh, it means they're nervous.

standing with one foot locked around the back of the knee it's called a foot-lock – they're shy and nervous.

slapping the outside of their thighs as one big gesture, jocularity. Tiny, repeated slaps mean they want to leave.

shuffling feet, twitching toes the person is nervous and could be lying.